EDUCATION AND THE LEGAL STRUCTURE

Harvard
Educational
Review

Reprint
Series No. 6

First printing, 1971
Library of Congress Catalog Card Number 79-166217
Printed in the United States of America

Harvard Educational Review
Longfellow Hall, 13 Appian Way
Cambridge, Massachusetts 02138

EDUCATION AND THE LEGAL STRUCTURE

The Poor, the Schools, and Equal Protection

DAVID L. KIRP

Harvard University

This article considers the state's duty to afford equal educational opportunity in light of (1) the Coleman Report and its progeny, and (2) landmark judicial decisions of the past decade concerned with the meaning of "equal protection," where "fundamental rights" are at stake. The article develops a set of standards for identifying fundamental rights and applies this fundamental rights analysis to public education. Based on that analysis, the article asserts that the state has a vastly greater constitutional obligation to its schoolchildren than it presently accepts. It proposes judicial tests of the implications of that expanded obligation.

While educators have long spoken of equality of educational opportunity, it has been tacitly understood for at least as long that the quality of education that a schoolchild received depended in large part on the community in which he happened to grow up. Suburban towns have had sufficient financial resources to afford the finest facilities and the best qualified teachers; their students have come almost exclusively from upper middle-class backgrounds. In contrast, at least since World War II, the big cities have been poor cities, poor both in money available to spend for facilities and teachers, and in vitally important human resources. This disparity between rich suburbs and poor cities (and rural poverty areas in

Harvard Educational Review   Vol. 38   No. 4   Fall 1968, 635-668

places such as Appalachia) has, through longevity, acquired the aura of inevitability. Yet from a constitutional standpoint, the inevitability of the status quo is far less clear.

The pertinent constitutional provision upon which poor cities might pin their hopes in challenging the status quo is the equal protection clause of the Fourteenth Amendment. That provision, addressed to the states, is brief and seemingly unambiguous: "No state shall . . . deny to any person within its jurisdiction the equal protection of the laws." The meaning of that requirement has, however, varied when tested in different contexts by the courts.

Traditional constitutional analysis has left the state ample leeway to adopt social legislation that benefited different segments of the community unequally. In certain areas, however—notably criminal process and suffrage—the Court has read the requirement of equality more literally, as imposing an affirmative duty on the state to overcome inequalities caused by economic happenstance.

This essay moves from an examination of the rationale of these new equal protection decisions to a consideration of public education, concluding that criminal process, suffrage, and public education all bear so directly and fundamentally on the nature of our society that they require judicial analysis differing radically from traditional equal protection analysis. The state owes a vastly greater responsibility to all of its schoolchildren than it presently accepts. It is constitutionally obliged, not merely to open its doors to all comers, but to provide *effective* equality to all. A reconsideration of effective equality in the light of recent and extensive educational research studies, such as the Coleman Report, suggests that the state's obligation to provide an equal educational opportunity is satisfied only if each child, no matter what his social background, has an equal chance for an equal educational outcome, regardless of disparities in cost or effort that the state is obliged to make in order to overcome such differences.

The essay proceeds to a discussion of recent landmark cases which espouse this position, and suggests other lawsuits that could conceivably be brought (some of which are in fact in the preliminary trial stages) to test the implications of the expanded requirement of equal educational opportunity. The final section poses questions about the appropriateness, and the necessity, of judicial involvement in these complex, confounding, and critically important issues.[1]

[1] I wish to acknowledge, and to express my gratitude, for considerable assistance that I received in thinking through this paper from Professor Arthur Sutherland, Professor Frank Michelman, and Mr. Maurice Ford of the Harvard Law School; and Professor Daniel P. Moynihan, Professor Robert Binswanger, and Dr. David Cohen of the Harvard Graduate School of Education. Patricia Marschall and Sidra Stich assisted in editing this paper.

The Poor, the Schools, and Equal Protection
DAVID L. KIRP

I

Courts have long recognized that the equal protection clause could not be read literally to compel all legislation to have equal and universal impact. "From the very necessities of society, legislation of a special character ... must often be had in certain districts . . . . Special burdens are often necessary for general benefits."[2] The judicial wisdom has usually deferred to legislative expertise in discriminating between—classifying—persons affected. Courts have been satisfied if some rational relationship between a legitimate legislative purpose and the classifying principle could be established; they have not required a showing that the relationship be the *most* rational that could be conceived, that the alternative chosen be somehow the wisest.[3] Such questions, it has been felt, are "political," and thus inappropriate for judicial examination.

Only infrequently has legislation run afoul of the equal protection clause.[4] Where the classification appears to be based on pure hazard or caprice, where *no* reasonable classification relates the legislation to the persons affected, statutes have been struck down. "The equal protection clause prevents States from arbitrarily treating people differently under their laws."[5]

Statutes have also been overturned if they classify "in a way which is on its face rational, but which nonetheless proves on closer examination to include within a single classification some members not like others in the same group, or fails to include some that are like those in the group selected for favored or disfavored treatment."[6]

When a legislative classification bears on a vital personal right of anyone, regardless of his identity, that classification is scrupulously examined for reasonableness.[7]

When the legislature relies on certain traits, notably race and creed, in making classifications, courts have erected a presumption of unreasonableness. "All legal restrictions which curb the civil rights of a single racial group are immediately

[2] Barbier v. Connolly, 113 U.S. 27, 31 (1885).
[3] See, for example, Skinner v. Oklahoma, 316 U.S. 535 (1942); Tigner v. Texas, 310 U.S. 141 (1940); Heath & Milligan Mfg. Co. v. Worst, 207 U.S. 338 (1907); Bell's Gap R.R. Co. v. Penn. 134 U.S. 232 (1890).
[4] Tussman and ten Broek, "The Equal Protection of the Laws," *California Law Review* XXXVII (1949), 341, provides a cogent and carefully reasoned equal protection analysis.
[5] Harper v. Virginia Board of Elections, 383 U.S. 663 (1966) (Harlan, J., dissenting).
[6] McKay, "Political Thickets and Crazy Quilts: Reapportionment and Equal Protection," *Michigan Law Review*, LXI (1963), 671.
[7] See, for example, Carrington v. Rash, 380 U.S. 89 (1965) (right to vote); Skinner v. Oklahoma, 316 U.S. 35 (1942) (sterilization).

suspect. That is not to say that all such restrictions are unconstitutional. It is to say that the courts must subject them to the most rigid scrutiny."[8]

In the last decade, however, the Supreme Court has read the guarantee of equal protection more broadly, striking down state statutes which conditioned the exercise of certain rights upon the payment of a sum of money. Thus, where adequate appellate review of a conviction could be had only if a transcript was provided, the Court in *Griffin v. Illinois* found a denial of equal protection in the State's refusal to provide all indigent defendants with free transcripts.[9] In *Douglas v. California*, the state guaranteed appellate review of a criminal conviction. Those who could afford counsel had received a full hearing automatically; those who could not afford counsel had been provided free counsel only if, after an examination of the trial record, the appellate court concluded that counsel would be of particular value to the defendant or to the court. This provision was overturned by the Court.[10] In *Harper v. Virginia Board of Elections*, Virginia's poll tax, which conditioned the right to vote upon payment of a nominal fee, was found to violate the equal protection clause.[11]

These new equal protection decisions were related in several significant ways: the legislation struck down by the Court had put a monetary condition upon the exercise of a right;[12] those adversely affected were too poor to be able to make the demanded payment, and thus were effectively foreclosed from exercising the right. Traditional constitutional analysis prevented the states from expressly discriminating against the poor by preventing them, for example, from entering the state;[13] the equal protection afforded in these cases went further, compelling the mitigation, if not the elimination, of the impact of poverty in certain contexts.

---

[8] Koremtsu v. United States, 323 U.S. 214 (1944). Where legislation, though fair on its face, has operated to discriminate against a racial or ethnic group, courts have not hesitated to strike down the legislation. Takahashi v. Fish & Game Comm'n., 334 U.S. 410 (1948); Yick Wo v. Hopkins, 118 U.S. 356 (1886). *Cf.*, Strauder v. West Virginia, 100 U.S. 303 (1880) at 307-8:

What is this [Fourteenth Amendment] but declaring that the law in the States shall be the same for the black as for the white; that all persons, whether colored or white, shall stand equal before the laws of the States, and, in regard to the colored race, for whose protection the amendment was primarily designed, that no discrimination shall be made against them by law because of their color. . . . [that they shall be protected from] discriminations which are steps towards reducing them to the condition of a subject race.

[9] 351 U.S. 12 (1956).
[10] 372 U.S. 353 (1963).
[11] 383 U.S. 663 (1966).
[12] The use of the term "right" may appear question-begging; when one concludes that something is a right, entitlement to that right may follow. The paper discusses "right" following its examination of *Harper*.
[13] Edwards v. California, 314 U.S. 160 (1941).

Seen in this light, poverty was no longer "constitutionally an irrelevance."[14] The state was obliged to take affirmative action to overcome the effects of poverty.

The four opinions in the landmark *Griffin* case all treat poverty as the dominant motif. The Court focuses not on "rational legislative purpose," but on whether an individual is absolutely entitled to exercise the right to an effective appeal regardless of his financial capacity; on whether, conversely put, the state may condition the exercise of the right on an individual's ability to assume the bill incurred in that exercise. The Court finds that "the public aspects of criminal procedure must be the same" for rich and poor.[15]

To Justice Harlan, the vocal dissenter in this series of cases, equal protection has a "more limited scope"; it does not require the "anomalous result" that the state must make unequal efforts to compensate for differences in economic circumstances; it does not permit overturning a rational state policy which happens to treat some more harshly than others.[16]

Harlan's discussion of a "duty to discriminate"[17] evades serious encounter with what is an essentially moral concern, stated simply if sweepingly by Justice Black: "there can be no equal justice where the kind of trial a man has depends on the amount of money he has."[18] The Court's opinion in *Douglas* gave some substance to the scope of the state's affirmative duty. Merely affording effective review (which Illinois admitted was lacking in *Griffin*) was not sufficient, the Court found. The state was obliged to extend the same procedural courtesy to all defendants, regardless of their financial circumstances.

Griffin, Douglas, and related cases[19] have been praised by commentators as preserving the "essence of citizenship . . . We cannot conceive of a man as truly a citizen if he is too poor to have access to the courts."[20] Insofar as it is limited to criminal process, that praise seems too narrowly directed. As Justice Fortas has said:

The significance of these [criminal process] cases in terms of our national philosophy, goes beyond the criminal law. Apart from their specific meaning . . . they stand for the proposition that *the state may be obligated in some situations to bridge the gaps which in-*

[14] *Ibid.*, 184.
[15] Griffin v. Illinois, 351 U.S. 12, 23 (1956) (Frankfurter, J., concurring).
[16] *Ibid.*, 34 (Harlan, J., dissenting).
[17] *Ibid.*, 35.
[18] *Ibid.*, 19.
[19] See, for example, Rinaldi v. Yaeger, 384 U.S. 305 (1966).
[20] Willcox and Bloustein, "The Griffin Case: Poverty and the Fourteenth Amendment," *Cornell Law Quarterly*, XLIII (1957), 16.

digency has created between a person and his constitutional rights. They represent a refusal to accept the fact of poverty as relieving the state from an affirmative duty to assure that all persons have access to constitutional rights. They request the state to do whatever is necessary, even if it means spending state funds, to make constitutional rights a living reality for everyone.[21]

The right to vote is a second fundamental right of which the Court is particularly solicitous. In striking down Virginia's poll tax requirement in *Harper v. Virginia Board of Elections,* the Court again focuses upon the impact of legislation on the poor. The Court's holding rests on the importance of the right of suffrage, and not on the irrationality of state policy; the fundamental nature of that right restricts the state's usual freedom to set standards.[22] The Court substitutes reliance on the fundamental nature of the electoral process for the "equal justice" rhetoric of the criminal process cases.

The Court in all of these cases is seeking some standard by which to identify the spheres of public involvement that are sufficiently crucial—to the individual and to the community—to merit rigorous judicial attention. In those areas, the Court is abandoning its typical attitude of deference to the legislature and engaging in a balancing of personal and public interest not usually associated with equal protection cases. "The Court has in fact found state action to violate the equal protection clause where, *upon balance,* the good or benefit reasonably to be accomplished for society by the state action fails to outweigh the harm or deprivation imposed upon those individuals unfavorably classified."[23]

In its examination of these measures, the Court may look for evidence of the conventional wisdom, of what the community regards as appropriate and proper.[24] That evidence is relevant; it does not, however, conclude the inquiry. The patterns of the past need not be imposed upon the future; as Justice Frankfurter noted, "local customs, though hardened by time, are not decreed in heaven."[25] Some effort at comprehending fundamental rights that moves beyond the status quo is required, both to allay the fears of those who predict that inflexible standards will cause the demise of creative legislating, and to rebut the

[21] Fortas, "Equal Rights—For Whom?" *New York University Law Review,* XLII (1967), 410. (Emphasis added.)

[22] Hyman and Newhouse, "Standards for Preferred Freedoms: Beyond the First," *Northwestern University Law Review,* LX (1965), 78-79.

[23] Note, "Equal Protection and the Indigent: Griffin and Its Progeny," *Stanford Law Review,* XVI (1964), 399. (Emphasis added.)

[24] Note, "Discrimination Against the Poor and the Fourteenth Amendment," *Harvard Law Review,* LXXXI (1967), 439.

[25] Cooper v. Aaron, 358 U.S. 1, 25 (1958).

contrary assertion that *Griffin* and *Harper* are wholly unrelated instances of the Warren Court's liberalism.

An examination of what have been termed "ultimate values" protected by the law provides one way of identifying areas suitable for careful judicial equal protection scrutiny:

First, is *the value of man himself,* of the individual as a creature of dignity and essential worth. Corollary to this are *values of liberty and equality* which are nonetheless significant because it is difficult to define them with precision or determine their specific scope. Also basic to this value structure is some degree of the *material requisites of a decent life.* Finally, but not last among these fundamental values in the Judeo-Christian tradition, is *the opportunity for people to participate significantly in the control of their government.*[26]

These values, just as the values conserved in *Griffin, Douglas,* and *Harper,* are personal rights which permit a man to function with at least minimal effectiveness in the society; further, they assume that a certain economic standard, sufficient to assure "the material requisites of a decent life," will be maintained.

The values which merit expansive equal protection treatment may be defined in another perhaps more precise way by a slightly different set of standards.[27] *First,* does the right bear directly on the individual's effective participation in the political process? The popular nature of that process gives legitimacy to the coerciveness of the decisions reached through the process. A citizen's capacity to participate in the political process at some future time ought not be contingent on past outcomes of that process. *Second,* is the preservation of the right essential to the maintenance of the values of the society? In the area of criminal procedure, for example, one reason that a person may be regarded as having a claim to whatever is essential to his functioning effectively as a criminal defendant is because it benefits *society* that the defendant is able to function effectively in that role. *Third,* is the right generally considered essential for the individual's satisfactory life prospects?

These three measures, taken together, do not describe a standard to be applied mechanically. Nor do they provide a static definition; what is fundamental will vary with the varying expectations of the society. As the Court in *Harper* states: "Notions of what constitutes equal treatment for purposes of the Equal Protection Clause *do* change . . . We have long been mindful that where

[26] Harvey, "The Challenge of the Rule of Law," *Michigan Law Review,* LIX (1961), 608-609. (Emphasis added.)

[27] The "fundamental rights" analysis owes much to Professor Frank Michelman of the Harvard Law School, who has raised similar points both in unpublished course materials and in discussions.

fundamental rights and liberties are asserted under the equal protection clause, classifications which might invade or restrain them must be closely scrutinized and carefully confined."[28] These measures are useful in suggesting a rule of reason that can be applied to determine what state services are in fact rights, equal access to which is assured to all.[29]

The recognition and identification of fundamental rights compels a different understanding of what equal protection entails, and what is to be regarded as discriminatory state action. The state "discriminates" in offering fundamental goods and services if the way in which they are offered leaves some people unable to afford them. Put another way: the pertinent question for the Court is whether everyone has an equal share of the goods, measured according to need.

This analysis is useful for several reasons. It gives fundamental goods, or rights, a more definite meaning, suggesting that at least criminal procedure and suffrage are included within this class of rights. Furthermore, it suggests a balancing test determination of "fundamental": how significant is the good or service to the individual? to the society? how costly is the good? Finally, the analysis identifies the favored class of persons as those who cannot afford the good or service.[30] This makes the poor a constitutionally preferred class whose claims for equal treatment are to be looked upon with sympathy by the courts; a class to which the state's duty of equal treatment is not satisfied by a public offering, at the going rate, of fundamental goods.

II

The right to an equal educational opportunity merits special judicial solicitude because education shares with criminal process and suffrage the attributes of a fundamental right. Education bears directly on the individual's effective participation in the political process; it is essential to the maintenance of the society's values; it is crucial for the individual's satisfactory life prospects.

The actual importance of education to the individual and to the society has not been extensively examined. It has long been assumed (almost as an article of faith) that education is, as Justice Holmes put it, "one of the first objects of public care."[31] It is presumed, for example, that education can provide the skills

[28] Harper v. Virginia Board of Elections, 383 U.S. 663, 670 (1966).

[29] Cf., Reich, "The New Property," *Yale Law Journal*, LXXIII (1964), 733.

[30] "Afford" is ambiguous. Is it to be tested by a mere declaration? by some indigency test? more broadly, by an inability to take advantage of a public good or service? The question is taken up in greater detail in Section II.

[31] Interstate Consol. St. Ry. v. Massachusetts, 207 U.S. 79, 87 (1907).

The Poor, the Schools, and Equal Protection
DAVID L. KIRP

that enable citizens to make intelligent political choices and thus participate effectively in a government that exercises coercive powers. As Alexis de Tocqueville once stated, commenting on the relationship between education and politics in America: "it cannot be doubted that in the United States the instruction of the people powerfully contributes to the support of the democratic republic... politics are the end and aim of education."[32]

The quality of education provided to communities or social classes within the society necessarily affects the entire society. What happens in the schoolhouse in a poor rural community has a hand in determining the public contribution that its residents can make; it also influences the impact that this community has on the economy and on the life style of the larger society. Sidney Webb writes of this in describing the mythical and blighted hamlet of Little Pedlington:

We cannot afford to let the inhabitants of Little Pedlington suffer the penalties of their own ignorance or their own parsimony, because the consequences fall, not on them alone, but also upon the neighboring districts, upon everyone who passes through this benighted area, upon all those who have intercourse with them, even upon the community as a whole, whose future citizens they are producing . . . If they are permitted to bring up their children in ignorance . . . it is not the Little Pedlingtonites alone who will have to bear the inevitable cost of the destitution and criminality thus produced. Hence modern administrative science is forced to recognize that we are all, in the plainest sense, "members of one another."[33]

Education is highly esteemed because of what is regarded as its profound and measurable impact on an individual's life chances. *Brown v. Board of Education* asserts the point more positively: "Education is perhaps the most important function of state and local government... In these days, it is doubtful that any child may reasonably be expected to succeed in life if he is denied the opportunity of education."[34]

Any attempt to measure the relative importance to the individual and to the society of publicly-provided services confronts irreconcilable differences of personal preference and economic analysis. Education can, however, be distinguished from other public services in several ways: it has a long history of high public esteem

[32] A. de Tocqueville, *Democracy in America* (New York: Vintage, 1954), pp. 329-330. See also Note, "Discrimination Against the Poor and the Fourteenth Amendment," which refers to education as "the very foundation of good citizenship."
[33] S. Webb, *Grants-in-Aid: A Criticism and a Proposal (1920)*, in C. Benson, *The Economics of Public Education* (Boston, Houghton Mifflin, 1961), p. 218.
[34] Brown v. Board of Education, 347 U.S. 483, 493 (1954).

9

in this country, dating at least to the Northwest Ordinance of 1787, which provided that "schools and the means of education shall forever be encouraged";[35] it has so typically been regarded a vital public service as to be compulsory throughout the nation; it may have a direct impact on the effectiveness of participation in a political system which makes priority choices among *other* public services for the future; it is more feasible that courts will order measures designed to equalize educational opportunity than that they will respond to demands for, say, an income equalization subsidy.

Education is thought to be most crucial to the poor because, as the American dream would have it, education can operate as a social equalizer.[36] Success in education, the assumption continues, is the traditional and most readily accessible route for the underclass to break free of the culture and condition of poverty, to take a place in the broad middle class of the society. If this view is accepted, failure in education becomes a personal tragedy. "Much as disadvantaged children may try to hide their knowledge, they recognize full well that failure in education is terribly final and for them spells the end of the American dream of progress through education."[37]

Recent research forces qualification of certain critical premises of this view. The poor have typically been unable to utilize the schools as social equalizers. As a class, they have suffered the worst schooling, by whatever rational standard is employed. Extensive sociological surveys of public schools reveal a disturbingly consistent pattern: poor children go to the most outmoded schools with the least motivated fellow classmates; they use the shabbiest facilities and are taught by the least capable teachers; they do the worst and may be looked upon by the system as capable of doing no better.[38] As a member of the Boston School Committee indelicately stated: "We have no inferior education in our schools. What we have been getting is an inferior type of student."[39] Furthermore, the number of years that a child spends in school may well be irrelevant to success in the society, measured in terms of income. "It is *not* the number of years spent in school that con-

[35] Ordinance of 1787, §14, Art. 3.

[36] See, for example, Wilson, "Social Class and Equal Educational Opportunity," *Harvard Educational Review*, XXXVIII (1968), 78.

[37] D. Hunter, *The Slums* (New York: Free Press, Macmillan, 1964), p. 109.

[38] See generally United States Commission on Civil Rights, *Racial Isolation in the Public Schools* (Washington, D.C.: U.S. Government Printing Office, 1967), chap. 3 (Hereafter cited as *Racial Isolation*); J. Coleman, *et al.*, *Equality of Educational Opportunity*, U.S. Dept. of Health, Education and Welfare (Washington, D.C.: U.S. Government Printing Office, 1966), chap. 3 (Hereafter cited as *E. O. Survey*); P. Sexton, *Education and Income* (New York: Viking, 1961).

[39] J. Kozol, *Death at an Early Age* (Boston: Houghton Mifflin, 1967), p. 60.

tribute to earnings—rather it is *what he has learned in school* . . . if one merely spends additional years in school without learning much, then subsequent earnings will not be affected."[40]

In short, the society values education highly, both for its importance to the individual and its importance to the society itself. Yet society has acted in a way that particularly disadvantages the poor, by providing them with measurably less than an equal education. In *Griffin v. Prince Edward County*, the Supreme Court hints that the fundamental importance of public education may render such treatment unconstitutional.[41]

Griffin v. Prince Edward County overturned the decision of one Virginia county, acting pursuant to state statute, to close the county's public schools rather than integrate them, and to make tuition payments to students attending private schools.[42] The Court manifested its impatience with a decade-long history of

[40] Hansen, Weisbrod, and Scanlon, "Determinants of Earnings: Does Schooling Really Count?" (Unpublished study, University of Minnesota, 1967).
[41] In the past, courts determined what educational opportunity meant only when faced with a claim that racial classification made the education available to the minority inferior to that offered to the majority. This stress on the adverse impact of racial classification has sound historical and practical roots. From its first Supreme Court examination in the *Slaughterhouse Cases*, 83 U.S. 36 (1873), the Fourteenth Amendment's safeguards have been read to apply with special force to state actions which discriminate against the Negro. The history of state-imposed segregation indicates that, at least in the South, separate—by whatever guise maintained—always meant *un*equal. Slavery gave way to Black Codes shortly after the Civil War; when the South was barred from using these overt caste systems, it turned to segregation, and imposed that regime upon the Negro "to maintain and further 'white supremacy'" (Black, "The Lawfulness of the Segregation Decision," *Yale Law Journal*, LXIX (1959), 426).
Discriminations which adversely affect the Negro raise political and moral questions of crisis dimension. See *Report of the Advisory Commission on Civil Disorders* (New York: Dutton, 1968). The profound social, psychological, and material harm caused by such discrimination requires that courts continue to treat Negroes as a constitutionally favored group. See Black, "Foreward: 'State Action,' Equal Protection, and California's Proposition 14," *Harvard Law Review*, LXXXI (1967), 69. When examining public schools, for example, the impact of state-condoned racial isolation on the Negro merits close judicial scrutiny; in defending such a policy, school boards should be required to show not only that the policy being followed is rational, but that no other alternative is feasible. See Horowitz, "Unseparate but Unequal: The Emerging Fourteenth Amendment Issue in Public School Education," *U.C.L.A. Law Review*, XIII (1965), 1147. The related issue, whether *de facto* segregation is barred absolutely by the Equal Protection Clause, has been much discussed. See, for example, Fiss, "Racial Imbalance in the Public Schools: The Constitutional Concepts," *Harvard Law Review*, LXXVIII (1965), 564; Wright, "Public School Desegregation: Legal Remedies for *De Facto* Segregation," *Western Reserve Law Review*, XVI (1965), 478; Kaplan, "Segregation, Litigation, and the Schools," *Northwestern University Law Review*, LVIII (1963), 157; *Northwestern University Law Review*, LIX (1964), 121; Sedler, "School Segregation in the North and West: Legal Aspects," *St. Louis University Law Journal*, VII (1963), 228.
[42] 337 U.S. 218 (1964). *Accord*, Hall v. St. Helene Parish School Board, 197 F. Supp. 649 (E.D. La. 1961), *aff'd*, 287 F.2d 326 (5th Cir. 1961), *aff'd*, 368 U.S. 515 (1962).

Virginia's resistance to, and evasion of, the 1954 desegregation mandate. The decision, striking down Virginia's statute, appeared to rest on a finding of constitutionally forbidden discriminatory motivation.

Motive presents a slippery judicial test, one traditionally regarded as irrelevant to a consideration of an act's constitutionality: it is difficult to ascertain and susceptible to a range of interpretation.[43] In this case, bad motive is not altogether apparent. Virginia may have had a legitimate end in mind: to maximize local self-control by permitting each locality to choose the type of educational facility it wished to provide.

Such state motivation in perfectly acceptable in a host of other situations, including the licensing of liquor distributors and the operation of public recreation facilities.[44] The fundamental importance of public education compelled a distinction and led the Court to the extraordinary remedy of ordering the county to levy taxes sufficient to reopen the public schools.[45]

In *Griffin,* not all of the county's schoolchildren were injured in any meaningful way by the school closing. Students able to attend private schools, supported by state tuition payments, may have fared as well as their counterparts in other counties. Just as in the criminal process and poll tax cases, it was the poor—especially the Negroes—who were injured. No school served that class of children; the county's action effectively deprived them of any education for five years. Such a consequence, *Griffin* indicates, is not constitutionally permissible. Once the state undertakes to provide education, the right "must be available to all on equal terms."[46] That an ostensibly equal offering operates in fact to injure a particular class is sufficient to condemn the arrangement without any further showing. *Griffin* suggests a vastly expanded role for the courts in considering alleged deprivations of equal educational opportunity.

III

In this country, the concept of educational opportunity has had almost from the beginning a special meaning which implied equality of opportunity. The basic

[43] Cf., Fletcher v. Peck, 10 U.S. (6 Cranch) 87 (1810). For a discussion of the relevance of motive in school desegregation cases, see Note, "Racial Imbalance in the Public Schools—Legislative Motive and the Constitution," *Virginia Law Review,* L (1964), 465.

[44] Cf., Tonkins v. City of Greensboro, 162 F. Supp. 579 (M.D.N.C. 1958); Palmer v. Thompson, 36 U.S.L.W. 2158 (9/19/67).

[45] 377 U.S. 218, 232-233 (1964).

[46] Brown v. Board of Education, 347 U.S. 483, 493 (1954).

tenets of that concept included universal free education to a given age; a common curriculum; and a common school (except in the South) for children of diverse backgrounds.[47] The concept made two basic assumptions about equality. "First, it implicitly assumed that the existence of free schools eliminates economic sources of inequality of opportunity...A second assumption implied by this concept of equality of opportunity is that opportunity lies in *exposure* to a given curriculum.[48] The school, this notion suggests, is obliged to be available, to make an offering; it is for the child to take advantage of the offering.

That understanding of equality of opportunity is still popularly held, and for almost a century it was tacitly accepted by the courts. Judicial analysis focused on what went into a school, on school facilities. The state's duty to provide equal educational opportunity was deemed satisfied if it provided the same caliber of facilities—schools, texts, equipment, teachers—in all schools. Equality did not necessarily mean one and the same; separate facilities could be provided for a class or race of children, as long as they were "separate but equal."[49]

The "equal facilities" standard had the apparent virtue of ease of judicial administration. A mechanical test of absolute equality developed: if School A, invariably the white school, provided a particular facility, then School B, the Negro school, had to do likewise.[50] Sixty years of overseeing the "separte but equal" doctrine proved it to be ultimately unworkable, for two very different reasons.

First, the separate schools for whites and Negroes maintained by law in most Southern states were by no means equal even in their most obvious and measurable characteristics. Per pupil expenditure for Negro students was forty to seventy percent of per pupil expenditure for white students in the Deep South; teacher accreditation requirements were different; facilities were of unequal quality; even the length of the school year varied between the white and Negro schools in a given district.[51]

Second, the Supreme Court came gradually to realize that equality was not fairly measured by examining facilities alone. Subtler factors, including the prestige

[47] The historical analysis is drawn from J. Coleman, "The Concept of Equality of Educational Opportunity," *Harvard Educational Review*, XXXVIII (1968), 7 (Hereafter cited as "E.E.O.").
[48] *Ibid.*
[49] Plessy v. Ferguson, 163 U.S. 37 (1896).
[50] See, for example, Constantine v. Southwest Louisiana Institute, 120 F. Supp. 412 (D.C. La. 1954); Carter v. School Board, 182 F.2d 531 (4th Cir. 1950); Wilson v. Board of Supervisors, 92 F. Supp. 986 (E.D. La. 1950), *aff'd* 341 U.S. 909 (1950); McCreary v. Byrd, 195 Md. 131, 73 A.2d 8 (1950).
[51] Kaplan, "Segregation Litigation and the Schools—Part II: The General Northern Problem," *Northwestern University Law Review*, LVIII (1963), 162-164.

of the institution, the composition of the student body, and the impact on those served by the school had to be taken into account in ascertaining whether attendance at School B really did assure equal educational opportunity.[52]

In *Brown v. Board of Education*, the Supreme Court rejected the "separate but equal" doctrine, and held segregated education unconstitutional.[53] Interpretations of the basis of the decision and its effect on the meaning of equal educational opportunity vary. *Brown* may be read as asserting that the use of race as a standard for determining who goes to what school violates the Fourteenth Amendment. Another reading of *Brown* sees the Court's decision as broadening the concept of equal facilities to include integration as one of those "facilities."[54] A third reading regards *Brown* as asserting that equality of educational opportunity depends not on facilities, but upon the effects of schooling, and that the harmful effects of state-imposed segregation on Negro schoolchildren's performance render that segregation unconstitutional.[55]

Efforts to extend *Brown* through judicial decision to schools in the North and West have generally fastened upon the first reading suggested, and on this ground they have sought to compel racial integration. These cases have not pressed for equalization of facilities even though the constitutional requirement of equal facilities would seem to survive *Brown*.[56] This relative lack of interest in equalizing facilities does not imply that inequalities no longer exist. On the contrary, differences in such readily measurable factors as per pupil expenditures within and among school districts remain substantial. "Nationally, Negro pupils have fewer of some of the facilities that seem most related to academic achievement. They have less access to physics, chemistry, and language laboratories; there are fewer books per pupil in their libraries; their textbooks are less often in sufficient supply . . . . So too they have less access to curricular and extracurricular programs that would seem to have such a relationship."[57]

[52] Sweatt v. Painter, 339 U.S. 629 (1950); McLaurin v. Oklahoma State Regents, 339 U.S. 637 (1950).

[53] 347 U.S. 483 (1954).

[54] D. Cohen, "Jurists and Educators in Urban Schools: The Wright Decision and the Passow Report," *The Record* (Forthcoming).

[55] "E.E.O.," pp. 16-22.

[56] Rousselot, "Achieving Equal Educational Opportunity for Negroes in the Public Schools of the North and West: The Emerging Role for Private Constitutional Litigation," *George Washington Law Review*, XXXV (1967), 714. If, however, facilities bear little relation to the outcomes of education, differences in facilities may be overlooked by the courts if other and more significant tests of equality are met.

[57] E.O. *Survey*, p. 12. See also Burkhead, Fox, and Holland, *Input and Output in Large City High Schools* (Syracuse, New York: Syracuse University Press, 1967).

The Poor, the Schools, and Equal Protection
DAVID L. KIRP

Several considerations account for the apparent lack of interest in pressing for equal facilities. First, the cost of such an equalization would be immense; at the time of *Brown* the nationwide estimate was two *billion* dollars, and the price tag has doubtless gone up since.[58] Second, it seems both practical and proper to assume that if Negro plaintiffs succeed in their stated objective of compelling more than token integration, the problem of resource equalization will resolve itself. When Negroes become a visible part of the public school constituency, with needs inseparable from those of the white children, the needs of both will be satisfied to the best of the school board's ability. Third, and most important, recent extensive studies, including *Equality of Educational Opportunity* (commonly referred to as the Coleman Report) and *Racial Isolation in the Public Schools,* indicate that equalizing facilities may not significantly improve the education of poor children, white and black, if those children are compelled to go to school in social isolation.

It appears that variations in the facilities and curricula of the schools account for relatively little variation in pupil achievement insofar as this is measured by standard tests . . . The quality of teachers shows a stronger relationship to pupil achievement . . . . *a pupil's achievement is strongly related to the educational backgrounds and aspirations of the other students in the school* . . . . Children from a given family background, when put in schools of different social composition, will achieve at quite different levels . . . . The principal way in which the school environments of Negroes and whites differ is in the composition of their student bodies, and it turns out that the composition of the student bodies has a strong relationship to the achievement of Negro and other minority pupils.[59]

The Coleman Report suggests that if equality of opportunity is to be defined by "those elements that are effective for learning,"[60] the Court's focus should not be primarily on school *facilities,* but rather on the equalization of *human* resources,[61] for these resources most critically determine the fate of the individual schoolchild. The Report indicates further that, although racial composition has some effect on school achievement, social class composition has the most significant effect, and is an essential measure of equality of human resources.

[58] See Estimate of the U.S. Office of Education as reported in Supplemental Brief for United States on Reargument, October Term, 1953, *Brown v. Board of Education,* 347 U.S. 483 (1954). A recent estimate places the cost of adequate compensatory education at "between $100 and $160 billion in the first ten years of such an effort," not substantially different "in the order of magnitude of the costs involved for school desegregation" (Cohen, "Policy for the Public Schools: Compensation and Integration," *Harvard Educational Review,* XXXVIII (1968), p. 135.
[59] *E.O. Survey,* p.22 (Emphasis added.)
[60] "E.E.O.," p. 18.
[61] The second reading of *Brown* suggested at Note 54, above.

The higher achievement of all racial and ethnic groups in schools with greater proportions of white students is largely, perhaps wholly, related to effects associated with the student body's educational background and aspirations. This means that *the apparent beneficial effect of a student body with a high proportion of white students comes not from racial composition per se, but from the better educational background and higher educational aspirations that are, on the average, found among white students.* The effects of the student body environment upon a student's achievement appear to lie in the educational proficiency possessed by that student body, whatever its racial or ethnic composition.[62]

A subsequent study of schools in Richmond, California, confirms these findings:

Allowing for variation in primary-grade mental maturity, *the social-class composition of the primary school has the largest independent effect upon sixth grade reading level.* Among students who attended schools with similar social class backgrounds, neither the racial composition of the school nor the characteristics of the neighborhood made any difference . . . . The achievement of white students who attended predominantly white elementary schools has been strongly affected by the social class composition of the school. *But the degree of racial integration of a school has no effect upon the achievement of white students who attended modally middle-class schools.*[63]

This modification of the underpinnings of *Brown* is heartening, politically significant, and of importance to the judicial analysis. It heartens because it reveals that what will most benefit poor Negro children is not the opportunity to go to school with poor white children (matching "dumb black kids with dumb white kids," as one Negro leader succinctly put it) but the opportunity to attend school with children who are better off—financially, socialy, culturally—than they are. (The needs of poor white children, it should be pointed out, are much the same.) It is politically significant, because to require the mixing of rich and poor, or underachievers and achievers, whatever their race may be, sounds more palatable than busing Negro children into white schools. In those areas where a large number of poor whites live, the results of a Coleman Report-inspired decision will differ significantly from the results of a *Brown*-inspired decision.

---

[62] *E.O. Survey*, p. 310. (Emphasis added.)

[63] Wilson, "Educational Consequences of Segregation in a California Community," in *Racial Isolation* (Appendices) (1967), pp. 180, 183 (Hereafter cited as Wilson, "Educational Consequences"). (Emphasis added.) See also P. Sexton, *Education and Income*. Wilson does credit racial composition with some effect on school achievement. He points out that "while race, along with social class has a differentiating effect upon pre-school development, it has no continuing additive effect during the elementary school years. . . . it has a large renewed effect when students enter junior high school" (Wilson, "Educational Consequences," p. 182).

Most important, these findings confront the courts with the need to articulate in terms more precise than those used in *Brown* what equal educational opportunity requires. Coleman himself suggests five possible different measures: (1) facilities—school plant, per pupil expenditure, quality of teachers; (2) racial composition of the school; (3) intangible factors—morale, prestige, expectations in the school; (4) consequences of the school for individuals with equal backgrounds and abilities; (5) consequences of the school for individuals with unequal backgrounds and abilities.[64] Quite obviously, the different measures of equality stemming from the Coleman Report and *Brown* make different demands on the school system.

Equalization of the first three measures is the least that any court can demand, after *Brown*.[65] These may well represent a consensus view of what the schools should be doing. Yet the education studies discussed above reveal that these measures are inadequate if *effective* equal opportunity is sought. Measures (4) and (5) imply an *outcomes*-test of equality, and not an equal *facilities* test.[66] Measure (5) places a further burden on the school; in effect, it calls upon the school to create achievement, overcoming the effects of the external environment on its students. "The schools are successful only insofar as they reduce the dependence of a child's opportunities upon his social origins. . . . *Thus, equality of educational opportunity implies, not merely 'equal' schools, but equally effective schools, whose influences will overcome the differences in starting point of children from different social groups.*"[67]

Measures (4) and (5) define equality of opportunity as an end toward which schools should be aiming; just as in the criminal process and suffrage cases, no clear and exact standard can be asserted:

In this perspective, complete equality of opportunity can be reached only if all the divergent out-of-school influences vanish, a condition that would arise only in the event of boarding schools; given the existing divergent influences, equality of opportunity can only be approached and never fully reached. The concept becomes one of degree of proximity to equality of opportunity. This proximity is determined, then, not merely by the *equality* of educational inputs, but by the *intensity* of the school's influences relative to the external divergent influences. That is, equality of output is not so much determined by equality of resource inputs, but by the power of those resources in bringing about achievement.[68]

[64] "E.E.O.," pp. 16-17.
[65] Cf., Note 52 above.
[66] The third reading of *Brown* suggested at Note 55, above.
[67] Coleman, "Equal Schools or Equal Students?" *The Public Interest* (Summer, 1966) p. 72.
[68] "E.E.O.," pp. 21-22.

To focus on "effective" equal opportunity does not of course imply that everyone has a "constitutional right" to perform at the same scholastic level, or to earn an equal share of *A* grades and teachers' commendations, or to be admitted to Harvard. Students are not all equally intelligent; they vary in aptitude and ability.[69] Stressing the effectiveness of equal educational opportunity does however suggest that the school is obliged to exert its energies in overcoming initial differences that stem from variations in background, in home life (or lack of home life) and community.

In the past, schools have not been required to bring about achievement; they have long been thought of as "relatively passive . . . expected to provide a set of free public resources."[70] Yet when discussing other fundamental rights, criminal process and suffrage, the Court has recognized that the state does not satisfy its constitutional responsibility if it merely takes people as it finds them, setting equal standards of access. The state must assure each citizen effective utilization of the fundamental right, regardless of the disparity of effort that must be made to assure that utilization. This "effective utilization" standard varies with the different rights: the state is obliged to provide effective access to the criminal process; to assure the right to vote; to secure an equal chance for an equal educational outcome.

The word "opportunity" has ordinarily meant in the past that a facility was available, but that it was up to the individual to take advantage of the opportunity. The notion is that of a banquet offered, but the individual must serve himself. Our current concern with "equality of opportunity" seems to be introducing a higher type of morality that says that when soup is being served, those initially equipped with forks [or with no utensil at all] should be provided with spoons.[71]

[69] Stodolsky and Lesser suggest that "there may be patterns of attributes (cognitive, personality, motivational, and so forth) which are related in some regular way to ethnic group membership." (S. Stodolsky and G. Lesser, "Learning Patterns in the Disadvantaged," *Harvard Educational Review*, XXXVII (1967), 587).

[70] "E.E.O.," pp. 21-22.

[71] Mosteller, "Design of Experimental, Field or Additional Survey Studies," in *Questions Raised and Excerpts from the Analysis*, Harvard Faculty Seminar on the Coleman Report (Unpublished progress report, 1966-67), p. 4.

In a provocative article, Profesor Bowles suggests that even equivalent achievement scores will only begin to approximate equality of opportunity in the society. He suggests a sixth standard: equal economic results of education. Bowles, "Towards Equality of Educational Opportunity?," *Harvard Educational Review*, XXXVIII (1968), 89.

Such a standard of equal opportunity places on the schools a burden that perhaps should be borne by the job market. *Piper v. Big Pine School District*, 193 Cal. 664, 673, 226 Pac. 926, 930 (1924), provides some support for Bowles' position: "The common schools are doorways opening into chambers of science, art, and the learned professions, as well as into fields of industrial and

IV

Almost without exception, lawsuits seeking to apply the rationale of *Brown v. Board of Education* outside the South have challenged the pupil placement policies followed in a school district. The suits have alleged that pupil placement policy has had the effect of isolating Negroes within the public school system; that this isolation has denied to the Negroes an equal educational opportunity; that some remedy, typically school boundary redrawing, was necessary to prevent further inequities. The suits have stressed the fact of separation within the system and have not focused primarily on the wretchedness—the physical disrepair, the less tangible but more significant atmosphere of despair—that prevails in the ghetto schools. In cases of *de jure* segregation, where purposeful school segregation by school authorities has been shown, the challenge to the existing order has invariably been accepted.[72] The judicial reaction has, however, been generally negative where racial separation has been *de facto*, brought about not by provable design but adventitiously, by adherence to an arguably rational policy, most typically the neighborhood school policy.[73]

In at least two cases, alleged inequality of educational opportunity has been successfully employed by parents as a shield, justifying keeping their children out of school. In *Dobbins v. Virginia,* the state court found that "the physical facilities and educational opportunities [of the all-white school] are far superior to those offered at [the all-Negro school, eighteen miles away]"[74] and upheld the parents' decision to keep their children at home. In *In re Skipwith,*[75] an action brought by the New York City Board of Education to compel parents to send their children to school, the New York City Domestic Relations Court ruled that the substantially smaller proportion of licensed teachers in certain ghetto schools

---

commercial activities. Opportunities for securing employment are often more or less dependent upon the rating which a youth, as a pupil of our public institutions, has received in his school work. These are rights and privileges that cannot be denied."

[72] See, for example, Taylor v. Board of Education, 195 F. Supp. 231 (S.D.N.Y. 1961), *aff'd* 294 F.2d 36 (2d Cir. 1961), *cert. denied* 368 U.S. 940 (1961); Jackson v. Pasadena City School District, 59 Cal. 2d 876, 382 P.2d 878 (1963).

[73] See, for example, Deal v. Cincinnati, 369 F.2d 55 (6th Cir. 1966), *cert. denied,* 36 U.S.L.W. 3138 (10/10/67); Gilliam v. School Board, 345 F.2d 325 (4th Cir. 1965), *vacated and remanded on other grounds,* 372 U.S. 103 (1965); Downs v. Board of Education, 336 F.2d 988 (10th Cir. 1964), *cert. denied,* 380 U.S. 914 (1965); Bell v. Gary, 324 F.2d 209 (7th Cir. 1963), *cert. denied,* 377 U.S. 924 (1964). But see Barksdale v. Springfield School Committee, 237 F. Supp. 543, (1965), *vacated on other grounds,* 348 F.2d 261 (1st Cir. 1965); Blocker v. Board of Education, 226 F. Supp. 208 (E.D.N.Y. 1962).

[74] 198 Va. 697, 699, 96 S.E.2d 154, 156 (1957).

[75] 14 Misc.2d 325, 180 N.Y.S.2d 852 (Dom. Rel. Ct. 1958).

rendered them inferior to predominantly white schools and upheld the parents' right not to send their children to the assigned ghetto school. While the Court heard educators and psychologists testify to the harmful impact of segregation, the opinion relies almost entirely on a single statistic showing that the school in question had unlicensed teachers filling 43 of 85 positions, a proportion substantially greater than the city-wide average. The Court based its decision on that finding alone; it explicitly rejected the argument that *de facto* segregation is unconstitutional.[76] The board of education's contentions—that it bore no responsibility for voluntary teacher choices; that it could not coerce teacher placement and still compete with neighboring suburban systems for teacher talent—were summarily dismissed.[77]

For a host of reasons, the *Skipwith* technique of asserting a denial of equal educational opportunity is unsatisfactory. First, it encourages parental action fundamentally inconsistent with the educational goals sought; keeping a child home may have dramatic impact, but it diminishes the child's chances for *some* kind of an education.[78] Second, the approach leaves to the Domestic Relations Court, whose competence is usually thought to be more limited, the necessity of making decisions which will have city-wide impact. Some more appropriate tribunal should be sought out. Third, it requires costly and wasteful relitigation of the same questions; the board of education, which brings the suit, can presumably limit any action to a single school, if not to a single child. Fourth, to keep a child home from school is a dubious sanction for the school system, which could conceivably decide not to force the child to return to school, thus evading any judicial confrontation.

The major objection to the *Skipwith* technique is that it bases a decision of potentially far-reaching impact on a showing of inequality of a single measure of a single resource. That measure might well not be a meaningful one. The board of education might have argued (but for obvious reasons did not argue) that unlicensed teachers tend to be better teachers because they are younger, more responsive, less given to a hardening of the categories. The board of education might also have shown that it was compensating for the teacher disparities by other expenditures for, say, compensatory educational programs or computer-aided in-

[76] *Ibid.* at 336, 180 N.Y.S.2d at 864.
[77] *Ibid.* at 344, 180 N.Y.S.2d at 871.
[78] "For those children whose family and neighborhood are educationally disadvantaged, it is important to replace this family environment as much as possible with an educational environment —by starting school at an earlier age, and by having a school which begins very early in the day and ends very late" (Coleman, "Equal Schools or Equal Students?," p. 74).

struction. The single factor approach of *Skipwith* appears to foreclose this option, and with it flexible educational planning.

Hobson v. Hansen[79] represents a very different approach to equal educational opportunity litigation. In an exhaustive opinion[80] touching on numerous practices and policies of the Washington, D.C. school system, the District Court upheld the claim of the Negro and poor white plaintiffs to a wide variety of remedies. These remedies include revisions in pupil and teacher assignment practices; changes in the current building program; abolition of the existing tracking system, a technique for grouping students according to a tested measure of their ability; requiring compensatory education "at least to overcome the detriment of segregation and thus provide, as nearly as possible, equal educational opportunity to all school-children." The Court also ordered the school system to undertake metropolitan planning, in hopes of inducing cooperation from the neighboring Maryland and Virginia suburbs.[81]

While the fact that segregation had been mandated by law in the District prior to 1954[82] makes the Court more willing to apply broad remedies,[83] reliance on the prior *de jure* segregation as justification for the new opinion is expressly disclaimed. The Court is willing to hunt out inequalities of opportunity even where a showing of rational school policy-making can be offered.[84] While the Court shows greater caution in mandating remedies to overcome the adverse effects of *de facto* segregation,[85] the rationale of the opinion is not limited to instances of *de jure* segregation.

Skipwith stresses a single factor (the proportion of permanently licensed teachers) in a single school. *Hobson* painstakingly examines those several aspects of the school system that seem significant, either because the factor has traditionally warranted judicial attention, or because it is deemed to have an impact on the effectiveness of the education offered. These factors include racial and social class imbalance among students and professionals in the schools, and the system's efforts to deal with that imbalance; equality of facilities; differences in per pupil expenditure within the system; the relative quality of the faculty in the predomi-

---

[79] 269 F. Supp. 401 (D.C.D.C. 1967) (hereafter cited as *Hobson*).
[80] The findings of fact and opinion of law occupy 118 pages in the reporter.
[81] *Hobson* 514-518.
[82] Bolling v. Sharpe, 347 U.S. 497 (1954).
[83] Cf., U.S. v. Jefferson County Board of Education, 372 F.2d 836 (5th Cir. 1966), *aff'd en banc*, 380 F.2d 385 (1967).
[84] *Hobson* 503-511.
[85] *Ibid.*, 515.

nantly white and predominantly Negro schools (quality being measured by the amount of advanced education and numbers of temporary teachers, for example); quality and adequacy of the curricula offered; the impact of the tracking system. In its fact findings, the Court borrows heavily both from the traditional "equal facilities" analysis and from the Coleman Report's stress on the importance of human resources.[86]

The Court finds a common thread running through both sets of factors: children in the poor and Negro schools fare less well in all respects than do their neighbors in the middle class and white schools. The one hundred dollar per pupil expenditure difference between students in the predominantly Negro schools and students in the predominantly white schools accurately reflects a difference in the quality of resources available, and in the results attained.[87]

Equally noteworthy is the recognition in *Hobson* that the right of Negroes *and the poor* to a decent education merits special judicial attention. The Court is clear that the disgruntled suburbanites' claim of unequal treatment could more easily be dismissed than could the claim of the Negro or the poor. The Court also asserts that the government has a greater constitutional obligation when public schools, and not some other public facility, are under scrutiny.

If the situation were one involving racial imbalance but in some facility other than the public schools, or unequal educational opportunity but without any Negro or poverty aspects . . . it might be pardonable to uphold the practice on a minimal showing of rational basis. But the fusion of these two elements in *de facto* segregation in public schools irresistably calls for additional justification. What supports this call is our horror at inflicting any further injury on the Negro, the degree to which the poor and the Negro must rely on the public schools in rescuing themselves from their depressed cultural and economic condition, and also our common need for the schools to serve as the public agency for neutralizing and normalizing race relations in this country.[88]

The Court recognizes only with some hesitancy the right of the poor to make a claim traditionally made by Negroes. Note the difference between passages (1) and (2):

[86] The Court finds as fact:
1. Racially and socially homogeneous schools damage the mind and spirit of all children who attend them—the Negro, the white, the poor and the affluent. . . . whether the segregation occurs by law or by fact.
2. The scholastic achievement of the disadvantaged child, Negro and white, is strongly related to the racial and socioeconomic composition of the student body of the school (*Hobson* 406).
[87] *Ibid.*, 437.
[88] *Ibid.*, 508.

(1) Theoretically, therefore, purely irrational inequalities even between two schools in a culturally homogeneous, uniformly white suburb would raise a real constitutional question. But in cases not involving *Negroes or the poor*, courts will hesitate to enforce the separate but equal rule rigorously.[89]

(2) But the law is too deeply committed to the real, not merely theoretical (and present, not deferred) equality of the *Negro's* educational experience to compromise its diligence when cases raise the rights of *the Negro poor*.[90]

In Washington, D.C., the *Hobson* setting, the passages are reconcilable. The Court is not called upon to distinguish the demands of the poor from the demands of the Negro; in Washington, the poor are almost entirely Negro. In such a situation, "effective *social class* integration requires racial integration."[91] The opinion's references to the special problems of the poor may be read as an effort to propose broader judicial policy.

When the rights of a disadvantaged minority, however defined, are adversely affected, *Hobson* places on the school system the duty of justifying its policies, showing that the justification outweighs the harm. "Given the high standards which pertain when racial minorities and the poor are denied equal educational opportunity ... justification must be in terms not of excusing reasons of this stripe but of positive social interests protected or advanced."[92] Placing such a burden on the school system characterizes the new equal protection analysis.

Public school boards must provide equal educational opportunity for all students. Neither administrative convenience, desire to expend funds for other purposes, limited demand, higher costs, nor similar considerations would necessarily make consequent inequalities in educational services the product of constitutionally permissible classifications. In each case, assuming a 'rational basis' for a specific inequality [the usual equal protection test] were shown, the controlling issue would be whether the school board can demonstrate that there are not other 'rationally based' means of carrying out its programs which would have less adverse impact on the children who are provided the lower quality educational services.[93]

The *Hobson* opinion expresses dismay at the familiar story of the adverse effect of racial and class isolation;[94] among the remedies it ordered are meas-

---

[89] *Ibid.*, 497. (Emphasis added.)
[90] *Ibid.*, 497. (Emphasis added.)
[91] Schwartz, Pettigrew, and Smith, "Is Desegregation Impractical?," *The New Republic* (Jan. 6, 1968), p. 27.
[92] *Hobson* 498.
[93] Horowitz, "Unseparate but Unequal," p. 1165.
[94] *Hobson* 498.

ures designed to undo the effects of segregation. In Washington, D.C., however, a court order limited in scope to integrating the city's schools would be most unsatisfactory. At the time of the trial, the city's school system was 90.2 percent Negro, and the percentage of Negro students was increasing.[95]

In Washington, D.C., constitutional theory (segregation is unlawful) and educational theory (the indigent schoolchild's chances are most significantly improved by placing him in a school where most of the students are from a higher social class) confronted and were stymied by a political boundary as fixed as a wall. No tinkering with school district boundaries *within* the city could produce meaningful class or racial integration. The Court sought to overcome this special handicap by ordering the diversity of remedies already recited, thus operating within the bounds of the feasible. There is little discussion of the nature of the equality that the decision secures; the Court recognizes that no single feasible remedy could yield "equality," and that intervention at many points is in order.

The Court's dilemma is apparent in the findings of an extensive survey of the District's schools commissioned by the system.[96] The survey expresses the belief that "the fundamental task of the District Schools is the same as that for every other American school system: to provide for every child, whatever his race, education of a quality that will enable him to make the most of himself and to take his place as a free person in an open society."[97] While it urges that each child "have the help he needs to reach maturity prepared to compete on fair terms in an open society," and that "the schools must furnish unequal education . . . to provide equal opportunity,"[98] the study also asserts, realistically, that "it would be absurd to deny or ignore the special problems that a racially isolated school faces in preparing its pupils for life in an open society."[99] Racial isolation cannot be overcome by exhortations, or by judicial hand-wringing. The pattern will not be altered "until enough Marylanders, Virginians, Washingtonians, and Americans are convinced that their interests will be better served by making the national capital area a well-integrated metropolitan community than by keeping it the white-encircled black ghetto that it is now."[100]

[95] *Ibid.*, 410.
[96] H. Passow, *et al.*, *A Study of the Washington, D.C., Public Schools* (New York: 1967). (Mimeographed.)
[97] *Ibid.*, p. 18.
[98] *Ibid.*, p. 191.
[99] *Ibid.*, p. 185.
[100] *Ibid.*, p. 186. The Passow Report does find one saving feature in the social composition of the District. It notes that "the presence of many Negro middle-class families of superior educational background offers opportunities available in few if any other large cities" (Passow, "Washington, D.C., Public Schools," p. 190).

The Poor, the Schools, and Equal Protection
DAVID L. KIRP

For the present, Washington, D. C., is an atypical case: a city lacking the mix of human resources that the Coleman study suggests is crucial to effective educational opportunity. In other jurisdictions, courts have ordered redistricting of existing school districts, and careful planning of new school districts, to assure a somewhat greater social mix in the schools.[101] These measures, however, only begin to remove the inequalities.

Suits against a muncipality can have only limited success, if the end sought is *effective* equalization of opportunity. The city may be compelled to reshuffle its internal priorities—to build new schools in places it had not intended to; to assign teachers and students to schools it had not planned to—but the jurisdiction of the city administration, and of the court reviewing the actions of that administration, stops at the municipal boundary. Only a mapmaker's line separates Great Neck, Long Island, from New York City; Brookline from Boston. But the parent in Poor City who chooses to sue the school administrator is restricted to the administrator of his municipality. He has no legal basis for complaining that the administrator in the neighboring suburb of Richville is spending too much money on Richville's students. The Poor City parent pays no taxes in Richville; he casts no vote in the elections in which Richville chooses its school board. While he can appeal to Richville to accept its just share of the social burden of Poor City's downtrodden, he can expect to encounter the same unresponsive attitude that the Maryland and Virginia suburbs display to Washington, D.C.[102] Should the Richville School Board be so rash as to think that it had a moral obligation to salvage Poor City's children, a taxpayer of Richville might be able to go to court and prevent Richville from making a "gift" of its public assets.

[101] Barksdale v. Springfield School Committee, 237 F. Supp. 543 (1965), *vacated on other grounds*, 348 F.2d 261 (1st Cir. 1965); Blocker v. Board of Education, 226 F. Supp. 208 (E.D.N.Y. 1964).

[102] In a few cities—Boston, Hartford, Rochester—programs which bus poor children (usually Negro children) out of the city's slums to suburban schools have been initiated. These programs, however, invoke only a minute percentage of the Poor City schoolchildren; the suburbs have been willing to make only that token effort which does not "dilute" the quality of a suburban education.
In Rochester . . . those being bused to the suburbs number only 220, out of a total Negro grade school population in Rochester that is close to 10,000. The children being bused have been carefully chosen for good past performance and high future potential. Even so, the majority of Rochester's suburbs are now resisting a plan to bus out a few beggarly hundreds of additional children . . . And in Hartford, Boston, and all other cases known to me of center-city-suburban busing, it is again the same story of a few hundreds, usually specially selected, out of the many thousands of children who constitute the true problem (Alsop, "Ghetto Education," *The New Republic* (Nov. 18, 1967) p. 20).
One possible, much-discussed approach to city-suburban cooperation is the creation of educational parks. Each park would include several schools, primary and/or secondary, offering a wider range of facilities and courses than any single school could offer. The park would draw on a metropolitan area student body. See *Racial Isolation*, pp. 167-183.

The usual judicial action brought by parents against Poor City or Poorville, seeking congeries of remedies called equal educational opportunity, will at best result in a more equal dispersal of insufficient resources. This "equal but insufficient" resolution is unlikely to appease the citizens of Poor City who began the action, nor will it greatly benefit their children.[103]

The state, and not the municipality, has the capacity to provide meaningful relief for inequalities of educational opportunity, and thus is the more logical governmental unit to turn to for relief. Constitutional and statutory provisions, judicial decisions, and long-standing custom all bear witness to the state's responsibility for public education. "Education is not a subject pertaining alone, or pertaining essentially, to a municipal corporation. Whilst public education in this country is now deemed a public duty in every State. . . . it has never been looked upon as being at all a matter of local concern only. . . . In this State, the subject of public education has always been regarded and treated as a matter of State concern."[104]

The state may, under a constitutional home rule provision, be free to delegate certain powers to its subdivisions. It cannot, however, free itself of the underlying responsibility for the success of the educational enterprise by "pointing to the distribution of power between itself and its subdivisions—a distribution which the state itself has created."[105] In *Reynolds v. Sims,* the Supreme Court rejected a justification for state apportionment based on factors other than population that likened political subdivisions within the state to states within the Union. "Political subdivisions of States—counties, cities, or whatever—never were and never have been considered as sovereign entities. Rather, they have been traditionally regarded as subordinate governmental instrumentalities created by

[103] The point has been made with reference to Boston's public schools:
There must be change. There must be change in school districts and academic practice. There must be change everywhere in this historic and now decaying system. But almost all the changes discussed are fragmentary, or symbolic or, in some instances, self-defeating. It is hard to reform a system in which most of the staff, most of the electorate, and much of tradition are against you. It is hard to revolutionize an ancient city, hard even to know what you want ideally to achieve (P. Schrag, *Village School Downtown* [Boston: Beacon, 1967], p. 131).
[104] City of Louisville v. Commonwealth, 134 Ky. 488, 492, 493; 121 S.W. 411, 412 (1909).
"Every state has included provisions for free public education in its constitution and general statutes" (*Racial Isolation*, p. 260). For representative cases, see People *ex rel.* Nelson v. Jackson Highland Building Corp., 400 Ill. 533, 81 N.E.2d 528 (1948); Malone v. Hayden, 329 Pa. 213, 197 Atl. 344 (1938); Grant v. Michaels, 94 Mont. 452, 23 P.2d 266 (1933); Piper v. Big Pine School Dist., 193 Cal. 664, 226 Pac. 926 (1924).
[105] *Racial Isolation*, p. 261.

26

the State to assist in the carrying out of State governmental functions."[106] As Judge Wisdom declared, in striking down a local option statute which permitted a parish (the county unit) to close its public schools:

The equal protection clause speaks to the state. The United States Constitution recognizes no governing unit except the federal government and the state. A contrary position would allow a state to evade its constitutional responsibility by carve-outs of small units. At least in the area of constitutional rights, and *specifically with respect to education, the state can no more delegate a power to discriminate than it can itself directly establish inequalities.* When a parish wants to lock its school doors, the state must turn the key. If the rule were otherwise, the great guarantee of the equal protection clause would be meaningless.[107]

No single remedy will be equally appropriate for each of the many actions that might be brought against the state which has failed to provide the equal educational opportunity sought by Poor City and Poorville parents for their children. No single measure of equal opportunity can be insisted upon. "The constitutional command for a state to afford 'equal protection of the laws' sets a goal not attainable by the invention and application of a precise formula."[108] It is appropriate, however, in evaluating the possible remedies that might be sought, to consider how each would bear on *effective* equality; in other words, how useful each would be. The most likely potential remedies—an adjustment of school district boundaries and a reallocation of state financial support—will be taken up in turn.

By enlarging school districts, the state (or its creation the school board) could diversify the social class make-up of its public schools. Such a remedy, the Coleman Report implies, would do most to better the chances of the poor, presently locked into predominantly lower class schools. Conceivably, a Poor City parent (or the Poor City school board) could seek to have the state redraw the boundaries of its school districts by creating larger districts with more equal tax bases. Such a solution would alleviate the fiscal inequality between districts; more importantly it would alleviate the inequality of human resources between districts,

---

[106] 377 U.S. 533, 575 (1964).
[107] Hall v. St. Helene Parish School Board. 197 F. Supp. 649, 658 (1961).
[108] Kotch v. River Port Pilot Comm'rs., 330 U.S. 532, 556 (1947).

In assessing potential remedies, this essay does not consider the role—present and potential—of the federal government in supporting public education. That omission is due not to any lack of appreciation for what the federal government could accomplish, but rather to the determination, in limiting the scope of the paper, to focus on the state, presently the largest single source of funds for schools (forty per cent). National Education Association, *Estimates of School Statistics* (Washington: 1966).

by creating economically and socially diverse districts and enabling the Poor City schoolchildren to go to school in a heterogeneous environment.[109]

A requirement that the state take affirmative action to alleviate natural and inevitable differences (or so the state will argue) raises novel constitutional problems. Where the state's redrawing of political boundaries has resulted in discriminatory treatment of an indentifiable group, the Court has ordered the state to resurrect the former boundaries.[110] But the theory of the "equal opportunity" suit rests on a long-standing discrimination, not a newly created one; conceivably the Court might be more hesitant to upset established practice than to reject a discriminatory innovation.

The reapportionment cases provide a most tempting analogy. In the reapportionment cases, as in the hypothetical Poorville redistricting suit, affirmative relief—in both cases, the redrawing of a political boundary—is sought. Those cases like the "equal opportunity" case involve "civil rights," rights that the Court is particularly solicitous of. The reapportionment cases required redistricting so that "as nearly as is practicable one man's vote in a Congressional election is to be worth as much as another's;"[111] in the hypothetical action, a rough measure of equal outcomes would probably be the standard sought.

Yet the two instances are not identical. The reapportionment cases compelled redistricting because no other remedy could overcome the effect of disparities between districts or could overturn the rural dominance of the state legislature. In education, the availability of other, more traditional remedies, notably, increased financial support, may make the Court reluctant to insist upon school redistricting.

The Court concluded, in deciding the reapportionment cases, that the equal protection clause required apportionment of state and congressional voting districts on a population basis. That reading of equal protection was not the only way that equality could be understood.

In *Reynolds v. Sims*, for example, Mr. Justice Warren declared that "the right to vote" was "diluted," "debased," and "impaired" by unequal apportionment. But as Mr. Justice Frankfurter suggested in his dissent in *Baker v. Carr*, such a view assumes its conclusion: "one cannot speak of 'debasement' or 'dilution' of a value of the vote until there is first

[109] Professor Benson states that school districts should be no smaller than 250,000 if they are to provide adequate school services. C. Benson, *The Cheerful Prospect* (Boston: Houghton Mifflin, 1965) p. 45.

[110] Gomillion v. Lightfoot, 364 U.S. 339 (1960); cf., Wright v. Rockefeller, 376 U.S. 52 (1964).

[111] Wesbery v. Sanders, 376 U.S. 1, 7-8 (1964); *accord*. Schaefer v. Thomson, 240 F. Supp. 247 (D. Wyo. 1964).

defined a standard of reference as to what a vote should be worth. What is actually asked of the Court . . . is to choose among competing bases of representation—ultimately, really, among competing themes of political philosophy . . .[112]

The "political philosophy" that the Court chose to adopt views equal protection as requiring an equally effective vote: "Full and effective participation by all citizens in state government requires . . . that each citizen have an equally effective voice in the election of members of the state legislature."[113] The *equally effective* standard is also the theoretical underpinning of the hypothetical school redistricting action. Only if Poor City's schoolchildren can break free of their environment, will they have an equal chance to compete effectively—and to succeed in the competition. The importance of the right involved, and the necessity of the remedy sought, may well make a school redistricting order palatable to the courts. When political lines rather than school district lines shield the inequality, as shown in the reapportionment cases, courts are not helpless to act. "The political thicket, having been pierced to protect the vote, can likewise be pierced to protect the education of children."[114]

In a pending New York State suit the NAACP is seeking to have the Wyandanch, Long Island school district, a small, poor, almost all-Negro district, dissolved and parcelled out among the several adjacent districts, each of which is larger, richer, and predominantly white.[115] Wyandanch presents a case particularly favorable to the assertion that the creation of larger and more heterogeneous districts is a wise approach: the district is presently too small to be economically efficient;[116] it can be divided among the adjacent districts without overly burdensome impact on any one of those districts. The anticipated judicial resolution of the Wyandanch case should provide the first test of the appropriateness of seeking to redraw school district boundaries in order to remedy existing inequalities.

A challenge to the equity of state aid-to-education formulas is a second way that a Poorville resident could state his claim of unequal educational opportunity. In-

[112] Note, "Reapportionment," *Harvard Law Review*, LXXIX (1966), 1242.
[113] Reynolds v. Sims, 377 U.S. 533, 565 (1964).
[114] Wright, "Public School Desegregation," p. 498.
[115] The NAACP sought administrative relief; their claim has been rejected by the New York State Commissioner of Education. A suit in the state supreme court to challenge the Commissioner's ruling is anticipated. *New York Times*, Nov. 16, 1967; July 26, 1968.
[116] A survey of New York State's school districts concludes that "size has a negative effect upon very small districts and upon very large districts" (A.D. Swanson, *The Effect of School District Size Upon School Costs* (State University of New York at Buffalo, 1966), p. 41. See also Benson, *The Cheerful Prospect*.

deed, in rural areas where distances between communities render regional solutions infeasible, an increase in Poorville's share of state school aid may be the only remedy that the state is competent to give.

State grants account at present for approximately 40 percent of the local school district's budget.[117] These grants are meant to serve several purposes: to reduce extreme differences in tax burden among local districts, to afford relief for local taxation, and to stimulate local expenditures.[118] The most widely accepted state aid formula asserts that "equalization" is its primary objective. "There [should] be an adequate minimum offering everywhere, the expense of which should be considered a prior claim on the state's economic resources."[119]

The effect of state school aid has not in fact been to equalize resources or capabilities. Some state aid is offered to all districts, regardless of their need. Even when equalizing grants are included, "states in seven of twelve major metropolitan areas are contributing more per pupil to the suburban schools than to those in the cities. State aid programs designed decades ago to assist the then poorer suburban districts often support the now wealthier suburbs at levels comparable to or higher than the cities."[120] Thus state education grants, designed in part to equalize expenditures, may actually serve to widen the gap that divides rich districts and poor districts.

One conceivable grant reallocation remedy would require that *equal facilities* be available to each school district. Such a remedy would bring about a major reallocation of resources, benefiting financially those districts with a presently inadequate tax base. Yet compelling equalization of facilities seems an over-simple and unsatisfactory resolution of the problem. If a low-level equalization were set, the formula would impose unfortunate limitations on school districts willing to make a more than minimal effort; in all likelihood, no district would be significantly better off. On the other hand, to require that there be available in every school district the facilities provided by the state's richest and most education-conscious district would place an undue burden on the poorer districts and on the state.

[117] Benson, *The Cheerful Prospect*, p. 187.
[118] *Ibid.*, pp. 223-224.
[119] G. Strayer and R. Haig, *Financing of Education in the State of New York* (New York: Macmillan, 1923), p. 173. A. Wise, *Rich Schools, Poor Schools: The Promises of Equal Educational Opportunity*, (Chicago: The University of Chicago Press, 1968) discusses the constitutionality of unequal educational expenditures in greater detail.
[120] *Racial Isolation*, p. 28.

Nor would equalization of facilities serve any recognizable meritorious goal of public education. If equal protection compels *effective* equal opportunity, the Coleman Report indicates that merely equalizing school resources will not do the trick; equal treatment is not a sufficient state effort. "Were we merely to raise the quality of the teaching resources devoted [to Negroes] to the level of that currently devoted to whites, we would significantly improve Negro achievement. Nevertheless, we would reduce the gap in Negro and white verbal achievement at Grade 12 by only a little more than a quarter. . . . Equal school inputs will not produce equal school outputs."[121]

Focusing on effective equalization—an equal chance for equal achievement—stresses the obligation of the state to make a greater financial effort in those school districts whose needs are greater because their schoolchildren are less well-prepared for school. The state has a constitutional obligation to develop schools which will compensate as fully as possible for inequalities of prior training and background. The cost of such an effort, seriously undertaken, will be immense; the result well worth the cost.[122]

The theory of state responsibility for educational opportunity is currently being advanced in several suits, including an action brought by the Detroit School Board against the State of Michigan, which alleges that the state's school aid apportionment formulas unconstitutionally deny Detroit schoolchildren an equal educational opportunity.[123] The basic formulas in the School Aid Act utilize only two variables in apportioning aid: number of pupils and state equalized valuation of property in the school district. The school board asserts that these formulas have resulted in "substantial disparities in the financing of public education, and, therefore, in the quality and extent of availability of educational services and facilities among the several school districts."[124]

The state aid formulas are in no way related to the needs of the different districts; they fail to take into account differences among the districts. The state aid

[121] Bowles, "Towards Equality of Educational Opportunity?," p. 95.

[122] The Passow Report estimated the cost of compensatory education at "three or four times the cost of meeting the educational needs of the child whose home environment has already done a good portion of the job even before the child enters school" (Passow, "Washington, D.C., Public Schools," p. 259).

The magnitude of the necessary effort may seem to some to represent an overreliance on schooling as a tool for social amelioration. While a court will not be able to choose among alternative social policies (better schools *or* better housing *or* more jobs, etc.) it may, by denying plaintiff's claim, tacitly express its reluctance to order a major readjustment of fiscal and social priorities.

[123] *New York Times*, Jan. 24, 1968. A similar action has been brought by Chicago parents against the state of Illinois. McInnis *et al.* v. Shapiro, No. 68-C-673 (N.D. Ill. 1968).

[124] Complaint, Board of Education v. Michigan ¶11 (1968).

equation considers neither differences in the quality of facilities presently available, nor differences in the cost of providing the same facilities in different parts of the state, nor the added costs of adequately educating disadvantaged children. The theory of the suit is that even equal expenditures in all districts would not be sufficient; that equally effective education should be the end sought; the burden of financing an adequate public education system should ultimately rest with the state.

V

The ever-increasing involvement of the courts in reviewing administrative decisions concerning educational policy has disturbed some commentators, who point out that judicially-declared constitutional doctrine tends to be relatively inflexible, imposing a uniform standard where such a standard may be plainly inappropriate. Furthermore, it is suggested that removing discriminations against the poor usually requires governmental expenditures; the courts are not equipped to undertake an examination of alternative approaches, to determine how public moneys can best be spent to maximize public benefit. A third concern is that courts will be reluctant to undertake the commitment of judicial energy necessary to oversee the implementation of a judicial decision; failure to supervise this process effectively may reduce the prestige of the courts.[125]

These doubts are not easily put to rest. Judicial success in desegregation cases has not been spectacular. More Negro children are in segregated schools today than fourteen years ago, at the time of *Brown*.[126] The reapportionment cases have been extremely costly in terms of judicial time, and the decisions have on occasion been threatened by congressional counterattacks.[127] Were one somehow free to select the branch of government best suited to resolve the problems of equality of educational opportunity, the judiciary would not be the branch picked. Massive inaction of the other two branches, however, makes the judiciary the instrument of last resort for the assertion of fundamental constitutional rights.

The courts should be aware of their limitations in reaching their decisions, and in framing appropriate decrees. Rigid formulas, such as *Skipwith* imposes, are

---

[125] Fiss, "Racial Imbalance in the Public Schools," pp. 564, 612-617; Note, "Discriminations Against the Poor and the Fourteenth Amendment," pp. 435, 442-443.

[126] *Racial Isolation*, p. 8.

[127] See Note, "Reapportionment," pp. 1228, 1231-1238.

not in order; what is needed is a careful, *Hobson*-type case-by-case determination of the needs, the constitutional requirements, and the practicalities. For all of its massiveness, the Coleman Report does not pretend to offer an answer, or even a set of alternative answers, to our schools' problems. The Report reveals how little is actually understood of the ways that children learn, and how overwhelming is the schools' failure to structure patterns of learning and mastery effectively. Thus, guidelines to govern school policy, patterned after the school desegregation guidelines,[128] cannot and should not be imposed on the public schools. However, proposals intended to make over (and make better) whole school systems, such as the Bundy Report's plan to decentralize the New York City system,[129] should be critically evaluated by the courts in light of the contribution to an understanding of "equal educational opportunity" made by the Coleman Report. It may well be impossible to create school districts which strengthen the "natural communities" of a city,[130] promoting a "sense of community among residents of (school) districts"[131]—the core of the Bundy proposal—and maintain at the same time the heterogeneous school environments that the Coleman Report indicates are the vital determinants of school achievement. In short, community control and social class integration may well be incompatible goals. This incompatibility—and the effect upon schoolchildren's chances for an equally effective education—requires careful assessment before the rush to make major changes in the structure and operation of a school system receives judicial blessing.

Courts cannot and should not attempt the task of running the schools. Should the judiciary intervene unduly in the operation of the schools, the very able people who ought to be finding imaginative ways of making practicable the equal protection standard will be driven from school administration. Yet school administrators cannot be permitted to erect pedagogical expertise as a barrier to *any* judicial action. The very problems that the courts are called upon to resolve result from lack of administrative attention and competence in the face of basic educational demands. If the administrator refuses to countenance any relinquishment of policy-making authority, another, more politically responsive person will succeed him. To achieve a viable working relationship between the courts and the school administrators is yet another reason for suggesting the need for judicial flexibility

[128] 45 C.F.R. Part 181.
[129] *Reconnection for Learning*, Report of the Mayor's Advisory Panel on Decentralization of the New York City Schools, 477 Madison Ave., New York, New York (1967) (referred to popularly, and in the text, as the Bundy Report).
[130] *Ibid.*, p. 17.
[131] *Ibid.*, p. 77.

in framing decrees, and for urging that school administrators have a hand in framing those decrees.

At the conclusion of his opinion in *Hobson v. Hansen,* Judge Wright speaks to this problem:

It is regrettable, of course, that in deciding this case this Court must act in an area so alien to its expertise. It would be far better indeed for these great social and political problems to be resolved in the political arena by other branches of government. But these are social and political problems which seem at times to defy such resolution. In such situations, under our system, the judiciary must bear a hand and accept its responsibility to assist in the solution where constitutional rights hang in the balance.[132]

If the judiciary accepts its responsibility, and acts with imagination and sensitivity, it may be able to show the way to the beginnings of solution, to make good the American promise of an equal chance for all through public education.

---

[132] *Hobson* 517. See Wright, "Public School Desegregation"; Freund, "Civil Rights and the Limits of Law," *Buffalo Law Review,* XIV (1964), 199.

Students in Court:
Free Speech and the Functions
of Schooling in America

RICHARD L. BERKMAN

Boston, Massachusetts

American courts have perceived the political aim of American education and have generally accepted a traditional disciplinarian concept of educational purpose. The recent Tinker *decision is a notable departure, however. After a discussion of the legal history, the author evaluates the* Tinker *decision and possible directions post-*Tinker.

American courts have for years been engaged in an unsystematic and usually superficial examination of the purposes of American education. The reason for any judicial attention to the subject is suggested in articles by Goldstein[1] and Langenbach.[2] Goldstein, in his functional analysis of the legal limits of school-board authority, notes that school-board power over student conduct extends as far as necessary to fulfill the board's function of educating the students in its charge. He divides this power into two categories: education per se and service as host to the students. Education per se is, of course, the primary function of the school. The ancillary host function embraces such responsibilities as maintaining the

---

[1] Goldstein, "The Scope and Sources of School Board Authority To Regulate Student Conduct and Status: A Non-constitutional Analysis," 117 U. Pa. L. Rev. 373 (1969).

[2] Langenbach, "The Power of School Officials To Regulate Student Appearance," 3 Harv. Legal Comm. 1 (1966).

Harvard Educational Review Vol. 40 No. 4 November 1970, 567-595

physical plant and protecting students from communicable diseases.[3] A similar analysis is offered by Langenbach, who concludes that grooming rules must be justified either as fulfilling a "purpose of education in terms of the individual" (education per se) or as necessary to establishing an academic atmosphere free of disturbances (the host function).[4] Common to both formulations is the recognition that courts must come to some decision on educational purpose in order to assess the legitimacy of exertions of schoolboard authority in the area of education per se. Hence courts have been continually forced to determine for themselves the purposes of education in America.

In general, courts view school boards as administrative agencies of the state and thus consider a schoolboard act proper if it is "reasonable." Included in the determination of "reasonableness" is usually some explanation of how the act serves a legitimate educational purpose. But the greater part of most decisions is devoted to declarations of judicial reluctance to scrutinize the activities of local school boards. As one court phrased it:

The courts have this right of review, for the reasonableness of such rule is a judicial question, and the courts will not refuse to perform their functions in determining the reasonableness of such rules, when the question is presented. But, in doing so, it will be kept in mind that the directors are elected by the patrons of the schools over which they preside, and the election occurs annually. These directors are in close and intimate touch with the affairs of their respective districts, and know the conditions with which they have to deal. . . . [C]ourts hesitate to substitute their will and judgment for that of the school boards which are delegated by law as the agencies to prescribe rules for the government of the public schools of the state, which are supported at the public expense.[5]

Judicial diffidence towards local school matters reflects the traditional American belief that education is a local concern which should be shaped and supervised by local officials. Courts usually pay only hasty obeisance to the question of educational purpose and almost always find that the regulation at issue serves some valid educational purpose. By and large, the courts faithfully repeat the platitudes of educational purpose current at the time.

A notable departure from this tradition of judicial timidity is the recent decision *Tinker v. Des Moines Independent School District*[6] in which the

[3] Goldstein, 386-387.
[4] Langenbach, 4.
[5] Pugsley v. Sellmeyer, 158 Ark. 247, 250 S.W. 538 at 539 (1923).
[6] Tinker v. Des Moines Independent School District, 393 U.S. 503, 89 S. Ct. 733 (1969).

Supreme Court extended the First Amendment rights of speech and expression to secondary school students. Implicit in this decision was a view of the purposes and methods of education different from that traditionally expressed by American courts. This paper will examine the traditional views and the ways in which these views were incorporated into court decisions. In addition, the new conception of education expressed in *Tinker* and the probable effectiveness of the *Tinker* holding will be explored.

The Courts and Traditional Conceptions of Educational Purpose

Public education in America was never seen merely as a means by which all could share the inherent pleasures of mental exercise and development. Intellection as an end in itself was secondary to the political goals of public education. Proponents of public education were more concerned with training citizens than with increasing scholarship. Many saw education as a means of taming and civilizing the anarchic instincts of the populace. Hence schools were expected to teach discipline and respect for authority. Since the schools were to nurture good citizenship, this also meant burdening the curriculum with moral instruction and patriotic exercises. Further, those who saw the establishment of a uniform national character as a precondition to the development of a stable citizenry gave to the schools the additional tasks of removing ethnic differences, fostering social equality, and eliminating highly individualistic conduct. In short, as De Tocqueville could observe in the 1840's, "In the United States politics are the end and aim of education."

The educational purposes perceived by the courts originated in this overriding political, rather than intellectual, aim of American education. The view that discipline and respect for authority were major goals of public education was frequently enunciated by the courts.

In *Pugsley v. Sellmeyer*[7] a school rule prohibited "the wearing of transparent hosiery, low-necked dresses or any style of clothing tending toward immodesty in dress, or the use of face paint or cosmetics." Appellant wore talcum powder to school and was denied admission. In upholding the action of the school authorities the court said:

It will be remembered also that respect for constituted authority and obedience thereto is

[7] Pugsley v. Sellmeyer, *op. cit.*

an essential lesson to qualify one for the duties of citizenship, and that the schoolroom is an appropriate place to teach that lesson.[8]

In effect, since obedience and discipline were major purposes of education, virtually all rules served an educational purpose since rules, by their nature, taught respect for authority.

In *Board of Education v. Purse*[9] a parent visited her child's school and criticized the teacher before the other pupils. The Supreme Court of Georgia upheld the expulsion of the child as a means of impressing upon the other children the consequences of disrespect for authority. The court noted:

Public education which fails to instill in the youthful mind and heart obedience to authority, both private and public, would be more of a curse than a blessing.[10]

It would seem to require no argument to sustain the proposition that an act of disorder in the school room, calculated to bring into contempt the authority of the school as well as the individual in charge for the time being, should be met with such punishment as would be calculated to impress the pupils with the importance of obedience and respect to constituted authority. Children are too much disposed naturally to look with contempt upon authority, especially when represented by a schoolmaster; and parents should be restrained from encouraging this tendency so dangerous in its nature to private and public welfare.[11]

The court treated the disciplinary measures not merely as neutral devices for maintaining an orderly learning environment but as normative principles themselves part of the content of education.

The court in *State ex rel. Dresser v. District Board*[12] took the same approach. Here two high school students, at the request of an upperclassman, took a poem which satirized school rules to the office of a weekly village newspaper which published it. The Supreme Court of Wisconsin upheld the expulsion of the students on the ground that the poem had an injurious effect on the discipline of the school. The court cited approvingly the trial court's determination that the expulsion was not an abuse of board discretion since it was for the good of the school and evinced "an earnest desire to counsel, admonish, and discipline the pupils *for their own good.*[13]

[8] *Ibid.*, 539.
[9] Board of Education v. Purse, 101 Ga. 422, 28 S.E. 896 (1897).
[10] *Ibid.*, 900.
[11] *Ibid.*, 904.
[12] State ex. rel. Dresser v. District Board, 135 Wis. 619, 116 N.W. 232 (1908).
[13] *Ibid.*, 235 (emphasis added).

A later expression of this attitude is found in *Byrd v. Begley*.[14] Appellant was expelled for violating the school curfew rule and defying other orders of the superintendent. The Court of Appeals of Kentucky in affirming the expulsion pointed out that the state was justified in maintaining a school system at great expense because

we are self-governing people, and an education prepares the boys and girls for the duties and obligations of citizenship. Neither the schools nor the state can carry on without rules or laws regulating the conduct of the student or citizen, and those who are taught obedience to the rules and regulations of the school will be less apt to violate the laws of the state.[15]

The opinion is notable for the purity of its political-utilitarian view of educational purpose. There is no suggestion that enabling all men to experience the joys of intellection and personal development might alone merit government support. Rather, the expense of public education can be justified only if education is seen as a means of citizenship training.

In a recent New York case, *Worley v. Allen*,[16] even teacher obedience to rules was made part of the students' education. The teacher, described by the court as "competent, and perhaps inspired,"[17] was discharged for refusing to follow the assistant principal's directive that lesson plans be filed two weeks in advance. The Appellate Division saw value in the rule as an aid to administrative supervision and assistance of teachers. The court also stressed the importance of conformity to rules in the history of formal education. Not content to rest there, the court continued, "the machinery by which formal education is managed is in part a discipline for living in a community, both taught to the pupil and binding on the teacher." The entire system of rules provides an "object lesson by which the teacher's conformity to common rules serves for the pupil's edification."[18]

The court's gratuitous statement on teacher compliance as an educational device seems to suggest that no matter how damaging a rule is to the teaching process, disobedience to the rule would be even more harmful to the broad disciplinary aims of the educational system.

Moral instruction as a legitimate part of the education per se function seems

[14] Byrd v. Begley, 262 Ky. 422, 90 S.W. 2d 370 (1936).
[15] *Ibid.*, 371.
[16] Worley v. Allen, 212 N.Y.S. 2d 236, 12 A.D. 2d 411 (1961).
[17] *Ibid.*, 212 N.Y.S. 2d, 236.
[18] *Ibid.*, 238.

to have been assumed by the courts. *State ex rel. Beaty v. Randall*[19] concerned a student who was expelled from school after punching a classmate in the face and refusing to obey his teacher's command that he accompany the classmate home. In a mandamus action to gain readmission the student's father asserted the order was beyond the authority of the teacher, oppressive, and humiliating. The court held the order proper and commendable whether its purpose was to punish or to lend the injured classmate assistance, and asserted:

The teacher of a school as to the children of his school, while under his care, occupies for the time being the position of parent or guardian, and it is his right and duty not only to enforce discipline, to preserve order and to teach, but also to look after the morals, the health and the safety of his pupils; to do and require his pupils to do whatever is reasonably necessary to preserve and conserve all these interests, when not in conflict with the primary purposes of the school or opposed to law or a rule of the school board.[20]

The court's conclusion that the order would have been a commendable exercise in compulsory contrition represents a recognition of the moral component of the education per se function. At the same time, the court at least notes that this aspect of education is subordinate to "the primary purposes of the school"— presumably the teaching of the Three R's.

In the *Pugsley* case[21] the court failed to question the propriety of a rule aimed at inculcating values of modesty in appearance, instead upholding the rule on the ground that it might serve some disciplinary function in the school.[22] A refreshing, but atypical, dissent does not mention the disciplinary aspects of the rule and seems to be directed at its purpose as a moralistic standard for modest appearance. It notes the appellant was over eighteen years old and,

a rule forbidding a girl pupil of her age from putting talcum powder on her face is so far unreasonable and beyond the exercise of discretion that the court should say that the board of directors acted without authority in making and enforcing it. "Useless laws diminish the authority of necessary ones."[23]

The notion that the creation of social unity and equality is a purpose of public education also worked its way into court decisions. The unifying process involved fitting diverse groups of Americans—particularly immigrants and the "unruly"

[19] State ex. rel. Beaty v. Randall, 79 Mo. App. 226 (1899).
[20] *Ibid.*, 226.
[21] Pugsley v. Sellmeyer, *op. cit.*
[22] *Ibid.*, 540.
[23] *Ibid.*

poor—to the pattern American educators and statesmen held in highest esteem: white, middle-class Protestantism. Judicial approval of the unity theme facilitated the process.

The theme of social unity is most prominent in cases dealing with anti-fraternity regulations in secondary schools. School boards and those states which passed anti-fraternity statutes argued their necessity on three grounds: fraternity members tended to be less studious because of the time they devoted to their group's activities; fraternities divided the loyalties of their members, who would then disobey school authorities; fraternities were undemocratic because of their exclusive membership policies. The courts were nearly unanimous in accepting the last argument. In *Burkitt v. School District No. 1*[24] the Supreme Court of Oregon concluded that a school-board fraternity ban was reasonable because fraternities "foster an undemocratic spirit."[25] In *Lee v. Hoffman*[26] the Supreme Court of Iowa upheld a statutory ban because, *inter alia,*

affiliation with a society, no matter how innocent in itself, still has a tendency to breed hatreds and jealousies because the society may exclude some while receiving others, that the tendency of such affiliations is to breed division and class hatred.[27]

In *Robinson v. Sacramento City Unified School District*[28] the court noted that the school board rule, if applied to adults, would violate their First Amendment right of assembly; here, however, the ban applied only to adolescents in their formative years and dealt with

activities which reach into the school and which reasonably may be said to interfere with the educational process, with the morale of high school student bodies as a whole and which may reasonably be said not to foster democracy . . . but to frustrate democracy.[29]

The only court to overturn a school board anti-fraternity regulation was the Supreme Court of Missouri in *Wright v. Board of Education of St. Louis*.[30] At the trial the president of the school board, a former circuit judge, gave the traditional three arguments for abolishing the fraternities. Referring to their undemocratic nature, he testified:

[24] Burkitt v. School District No. 1, 195 Ore. 471, 246 P. 2d 566 (1952).
[25] *Ibid.*, 246 P. 2d, 575.
[26] Lee v. Hoffman, 166 N.W. 565, 182 Iowa 216 (1918).
[27] *Ibid.*, 166 N.W., 568.
[28] Robinson v. Sacramento City Unified School District, 53 Cal. Rptr. 781, 245 C.A. 2d 378 (1966).
[29] *Ibid.*, 53 Cal. Rptr., 790.
[30] Wright v. Board of Education of St. Louis, 295 Mo. 466, 246 S.W. 43 (1922).

[T]hey apparently had a continuing influence in breaking down that leveling spirit that is so desirable in an institution like a public school where every boy and girl ought to be on a social level, and where they are not on a social level, if a selected few of them belong to a secret organization and govern themselves accordingly as boys of that age will govern themselves when they do belong to that kind of a secret organization. There was a great deal of complaint from the children who were less fortunate, and who were not admitted to membership in the organizations. The organizations are built up by selection, and from the selection of the few, taking in only those they may think are their social equals or who they may happen to like personally particularly well, too, mainly on a social or business opportunity basis. . . . Those are some of the reasons why the board felt that the fraternity was an undemocratic and exceedingly undesirable organization to have maintained in a public school sustained by public taxation.[31]

The court held the regulation unreasonable since it invaded the home of the pupil, and cogent proof had not been offered to show detrimental effects to the operation and control of the school. The court mentioned in particular the failure of the board to adduce sufficient evidence of a decline in scholarship or deportment among the fraternity members. It would seem that the court rejected, *sub silentio*, the argument that fraternities are undemocratic and therefore should be banned since acceptance by the court of that argument would not have entailed any showing of proof by the school board.

Attempts by the schools to eliminate individualistic behavior under the guise of helping students to adjust to society have also been ratified by some courts. Recent examples center around cases involving school grooming rules. In *Davis v. Firment*,[32] for example, the court denied damages to a student suspended because his long hair violated a regulation set up by the school's principal. The ostensible reason for the court's ruling was its finding that the regulation served a necessary disciplinary purpose, since long hair caused fights and distractions. In order to support its finding the court cited testimony of the principal that fights had occurred. The court went on, however, to quote approvingly the superintendent's statement at the trial that

gross deviation from the norm does cause a disruption of the learning atmosphere and can create an undesirable separateness among students. Furthermore gross deviation can be and has been dysfunctional in the social adjustment of children.[33]

[31] *Ibid.*, 45.
[32] Davis v. Firment, 269 F. Supp. 524 (E.D. La. 1967).
[33] *Ibid.*, 528.

The adjustment rationale surfaces again in the district court opinion in *Ferrell v. Dallas Independent School District*.[34] Here the court approved the suspension on the usual disciplinary necessity grounds and then went on to offer an educational purpose justification for the grooming requirement:

One of the most important aims of the school should be to educate the individual to live successfully with other people in our democracy. Since the school authorities, by legislative grant, control the public educational system, their regulations play a part in the educational process. This is but another way of stating that society expects public education to concern itself with building young citizens as well as teaching the '3 R's'.[35]

Until recent years courts accepted without question the active role of the schools in engendering patriotic feelings in American youth. This acceptance was crucial in the early decisions upholding compulsory flag salute. In *Minersville v. Gobitis*[36] Justice Frankfurter said,

The influences which help toward a common feeling for the common country are manifold. Some may seem harsh and others no doubt are foolish. Surely, however, the end is legitimate.[37]

The New York Court of Appeals in *People ex rel. Fish, v. Sandstrom*[38] asserted, "we require the children to go to school to be instructed, among other things, in patriotism."[39] The court stressed the importance of "public opinion," calling it as vital to the maintenance of good government as an army or navy:

In fact these latter can be destroyed quicker by public opinion than by the attacks of an enemy. The state, therefore, is justified in taking such measures as will engender and maintain patriotism in the young.[40]

Hardwick v. Board of School Trustees,[41] indirectly a flag case, suggests the wide latitude open to courts to determine the importance of various educational functions of the schools. Here appellant objected on religious grounds to his daughter's participation in the social and folk dancing part of the school's

[34] Ferrell v. Dallas Independent School District, 261 F. Supp. 545 (N.D. Tex. 1966), *aff'd* 392 F. 2d 706 (5th Cir., 1968), *cert. denied,* 393 U.S. 924.
[35] *Ibid.*, 261 F. Supp., 552.
[36] Minersville v. Gobitis, 310 U.S. 586, 60 S. Ct. 1010 (1939).
[37] *Ibid.*, 310 U.S., 598.
[38] People ex. rel. Fish v. Sandstrom, 279 NY 523, 18 N.E. 2d 840 (1939).
[39] *Ibid.*, 18 N.E. 2d, 844.
[40] *Ibid.*, 843.
[41] Hardwick v. Board of School Trustees, 54 Cal. App. 696, 205 P. 49 (Dist. Ct. App. 1921).

physical education program. After deciding that compelling the child to participate against her religious convictions violated the state and federal constitu-
tions, the court asserted that more was at stake than an abridgement of freedom
of religion. The school regulation also involved the right of parents to control
their own children,

to require them to live up to the teachings and the principles which are inculcated in
them at home under the parental authority and according to what the parents themselves
may conceive will be the course of conduct in all matters which will the better and more
surely subserve the present and future welfare of their children. . . . Has the state the
right to enact a law or confer upon any public authorities a power the effect of which
would be to alienate in a measure the children from parental authority?[42]

The court concluded that the state or school board could not interfere with the
natural and constitutional right of parents to control the upbringing of their
progeny, assuming the views of the parents were not "offensive to the moral
well-being of the children or inconsistent with the best interests of society."[43]

The court then went on to distinguish from the case before it a recent case
involving the expulsion of children in a neighboring school district for refusing to salute the flag. The father of the children in the latter case had asserted
that the flag ceremony was against his Bible teaching and that fostering patriotism in the classroom led to militarism. The *Hardwick* court dismissed the
possibility that the flag ceremony could offend the teachings of the Bible. As to
the militarism objection, the court thought it repugnant

to every idea and every consideration of the loyalty and love of our government and
political institutions so essential to the maintenance thereof. No government could long
survive in the absence of patriotism in the people living under it, and one of the first or
primary duties not only of the public schools but of every other educational institution
in this country is to inculcate in those who attend them the principles of patriotism.[44]

Had the court seen teaching patriotism as a secondary purpose of education,
much as it viewed social dancing as a peripheral part of the curriculum, and had
it shown the same solicitude for the interest of a parent in not having his
child salute the flag as it had shown for a parent's interest in not having his
child participate in school dancing, the flag salute incident would not have

[42] *Ibid.*, 205 P., 54.
[43] *Ibid.*, 54.
[44] *Ibid.*, 55.

been so easily distinguished. But this would be a great deal to expect of the court considering the concepts of educational purpose current at that time.

Tinker and Emergent Liberalization: The First Amendment and the Educational Process

In *Tinker v. Des Moines Independent School District*[45] the Supreme Court held that First Amendment rights, applied in light of the special characteristics of the school environment, are available to students. School officials may not prohibit the expression of one particular opinion without evidence that such action is necessary to avoid material and substantial interference with discipline or the work of the school.

The petitioners, three secondary school students, were part of a group of adults and students who decided to publicize their opposition to the Vietnam war by wearing black armbands during the holiday season and by fasting on December 16 and New Year's Eve. The principals of the Des Moines schools learned of the plan and instituted an anti-armband regulation which required removal of the armbands under threat of suspension. Petitioners wore the armbands and were sent home and suspended until they would agree to come back without them. Petitioners' prayer for an injunction restraining the respondent school officials and members of the school board from disciplining the petitioners was denied by the district court. The Court of Appeals for the Eighth Circuit heard the case *en banc* and divided equally. Accordingly, the district court opinion was affirmed.

Justice Fortas, writing for the majority, characterized the wearing of the armbands as "closely akin to 'pure Speech.' "[46] It was a "silent, passive expression of opinion, unaccompanied by any disorder or disturbance on the part of the petitioners.[47] Nor did the Court's independent review of the evidence reveal a reasonable basis for anticipating substantial disruption of the educational process.[48] Hence, restriction of the speech could not be justified by what was here an "undifferentiated fear or apprehension of disturbance[49] or by a mere desire

[45] Tinker v. Des Moines Independent School District, *op. cit.*
[46] *Ibid.*, 89 S. Ct., 736.
[47] *Ibid.*, 737.
[48] *Ibid.*, 738.
[49] *Ibid.*, 737.

to avoid the discomfort and unpleasantness that often result from the expression of an unpopular opinion.[50]

Tinker falls into the rather recently adumbrated category of cases involving the problem of the exercise of First Amendment rights in a public place dedicated to specific uses by the government.

In *Cox v. Louisiana*[51] the Court overturned the conviction of a group of Negroes who had conducted a demonstration before a courthouse in violation of a state statute which prohibited willful obstruction of public streets or the passageways of any public building. While the court voided the convictions on the ground that the statute could be enforced in a discriminatory manner, Justice Goldberg asserted that "The rights of free speech and assembly, while fundamental in our democratic society, still do not mean that everyone with opinions or beliefs to express may address a group at any public place and at any time."[52]

In *Brown v. Louisiana*[53] the Court reversed the breach of the peace convictions of Negro demonstrators who disregarded a sheriff's order to vacate a segregated library. The Court said the statute was deliberately and purposefully applied solely to terminate a peaceable and orderly exercise of the right to protest the unconstitutional segregation of a public facility. In a strong dissent Justice Black, joined by Justices Clark, Harlan, and Stewart, asserted that public buildings such as libraries, school houses, fire departments, court houses, and executive mansions were maintained to perform specific and vital functions which demanded "order and tranquility of a sort entirely unknown to the public streets."[54] Invoking Justice Goldberg's broad dictum in *Cox v. Louisiana*, Justice Black concluded that the First Amendment does not give

any person or group of persons the constitutional right to go wherever they please, without regard to the rights of private or public property or to state law. Indeed a majority of this court said as much in *Cox v. Louisiana*. Though the First Amendment guarantees the right of assembly and the right of petition along with the rights of speech, press, and religion, it does not guarantee to any person the right to use someone else's property, even that owned by government and dedicated to other purposes, as a stage to express dissident ideas. The novel constitutional doctrine of the prevailing opinion nevertheless

---

[50] *Ibid.*, 738.
[51] Cox v. Louisiana, 379 U.S. 536 [No. 24], 85 S. Ct. 453 (1965).
[52] *Ibid.*, 379 U.S., 554.
[53] Brown v. Louisiana, 383 U.S. 131, 86 S. Ct. 719 (1966).
[54] *Ibid.*, 383 U.S., 157.

exalts the power of private nongovernmental groups to determine what use shall be made of governmental property over the power of the elected governmental officials of the States and the Nation.[55]

Within months a case reached the Court which provided Justice Black with the proper scenario for gathering a majority in support of his "proper use" doctrine. In *Adderley v. Florida*[56] the petitioners were convicted of trespass after refusing to comply with a sheriff's order to move their demonstration from the grounds of the county jail.

Justice Black asserted that the sheriff, as jail custodian, had power

to direct that this large crowd of people get off the grounds. . . . The state, no less than a private owner of property, has power to preserve the property under its control for the use to which it is lawfully dedicated. For this reason there is no merit to the petitioner's argument that they had a constitutional right to stay on the property, over the jail custodian's objections, because this "area chosen for the peaceful civil rights demonstration was not only 'reasonable' but also particularly appropriate. . . ." Such an argument has as its major unarticulated premise the assumption that people who want to propagandize protests or views have a constitutional right to do so whenever and however and wherever they please. . . . The United States Constitution does not forbid a State to control the use of its own property for its own lawful nondiscriminatory purpose.[57]

Justice Black's most recent statement of the proper use doctrine appears in the *Tinker* case, this time in dissent, however. Justice Black reviewed the fact situation, stressing that the armbands caused comments, warnings, and teasing by other students and that a mathematics teacher's lesson was disturbed by arguments with one of the petitioners. In addition, Justice Black asserted that while the absence of loud disorder supported the majority's conclusion that the armbands did not actually "disrupt" the classwork, they "took the student's minds off their classwork and diverted them to thoughts about the highly emotional subject of the Vietnam war."[58] Iowa's schools, he concluded, are operated "to give students an opportunity to learn, not to talk politics."[59] Petitioners' activities "distracted from that singleness of purpose which the state . . . desired to exist in its public educational institutions."[60]

---

[55] *Ibid.*, 166.

[56] Adderley v. Florida, 385 U.S. 39, 87 S. Ct. 242 (1966).

[57] *Ibid.*, 385 U.S., 47-48.

[58] Tinker v. Des Moines Independent School District, *op. cit.*, 742.

[59] *Ibid.*, 745.

[60] *Ibid.*, 745, quoting Waugh v. Mississippi University, 237 U.S. 589, 596-597, 35 S. Ct. 720, 723 (1915) (upholding state anti-fraternity act).

Given this factual analysis, Justice Black placed the *Tinker* case in the conceptual framework erected in *Adderley*. The petitioners' behavior in *Tinker*, as in *Adderley*, interfered with the use of the property designated primary by the state: education. Thus, Justice Black could justify restricting the speech since

it is a myth to say that any person has a constitutional right to say what he pleases, where he pleases, and when he pleases.[61]

What separates the majority from Justice Black's dissent in *Tinker* is Justice Fortas' statement that "There is here no evidence whatever of petitioners' interference, actual or nascent, with the school's work."[62] In Justice Fortas' view the petitioners' activities did not interfere with the use of the property designated primary by the state. In fact, the opinion suggests, it might have brought about the fulfillment of that primary use. The difference between Justices Fortas and Black amounts to a disagreement over how to define interference with the work of the school, or stated more generally, how to define the work of the school.

Much of the dicta in the majority opinion suggest that the Court's opinion on this question represents a remarkable departure from the conceptions of the purpose and process of education incorporated in the court decisions of the last hundred years. There is first none of the familiar rhetoric about the disciplinary purposes of education. The extension of First Amendment rights to students means that in some circumstances courts will vindicate the actions of students who disobey the commands of their teachers. Justice Black is disturbed by this prospect and phrases the traditional argument as follows:

School discipline, like parental discipline, is an integral and important part of training our children to be good citizens—to be better citizens. Here a very small number of students have crisply and summarily refused to obey a school order designed to give pupils who want to learn the opportunity to do so. One does not need to be a prophet or the son of the prophet to know that after the Court's holding today some students will be ready, able, and willing to defy their teachers on practically all orders.[63]

Justice Fortas, on the other hand, in noting that the school authorities' fear of disturbance does not justify curtailment of free speech, points out that "Any departure from absolute regimentation may cause trouble."[64] In Justice Fortas' view the school which is open and willing to risk trouble better prepares its stu-

---

[61] Tinker, *Ibid.*, 744.
[62] *Ibid.*, 737.
[63] *Ibid.*, 746.
[64] *Ibid.*, 737.

dents for life in our "relatively permissive, often disputatious society."[65] Thus, the modern school can accept some disruption. Only if it is "material and substantial" can speech be proscribed.

While the *Tinker* opinion accepts the conventional view of education as a tool for citizenship-building, the type of citizen desired and the educational means of attaining this ideal differ from the orthodox conceptions. First, the majority recognizes that the process of education can be more important than its content in achieving educational aims. In the *Tinker* case the majority asserts that "state-operated schools may not be enclaves of totalitarianism. School officials do not possess absolute authority over their students."[66] The State may not regard students as "closed-circuit recipients of only that which the State chooses to communicate."[67] But the Court recognizes that this diminution of teacher authority will actually enhance the educational process, since

The Nation's future depends upon leaders trained through wide exposure to that robust exchange of ideas which discovers truth "out of a multitude of tongues, rather than through any kind of authoritative selection."[68]

Justice Fortas shares the progressives' belief in the student as a participant in the educational process. In *Tinker* the student is an initator, though here counterpoised against the diminished but extant authority of the teacher in order to insure controversy and freedom of exchange. Fortas, unlike some later progressives, is concerned with the effects of the educational process on society as well as on the child. He shares Dewey's faith in the beneficial consequences for society of an educational system which does not insist on imposing goals on the student and is more willing to permit the student to participate actively in, and exert an influence upon, the work of the classroom.

The thesis of the *Tinker* opinion is that First Amendment rights in the classroom are actually essential to an effective educational process in a democracy rather than a source of disruption of that process. Justice Fortas includes the First Amendment as part of the educational scheme; Justice Black sees it as an intrusion. The Fortas view is still political, but its antecedents are in the democratic conception of an enlightened citizenry possessed of the critical powers necessary to sustain a democracy. The Black view, political as well, reflects the

[65] *Ibid.*, 737-738.
[66] *Ibid.*, 739.
[67] *Ibid.*, 739.
[68] *Ibid.*, 739, quoting Keyishian v. Board of Regents, 385 U.S. 589, 603, 87 S. Ct. 675, 683 (1967).

conservative conception of education as an instrument of the state which actively works on students, disciplining them and teaching them patriotism rather than permitting them to become patriotic by experiencing the values which we historically associated with patriotism.

Elements of the *Tinker* Court's position on educational purpose have appeared in earlier opinions. In *West Virginia State Board of Education v. Barnette*,[69] which held compulsory flag salute unconstitutional, Justice Jackson stressed the *educational* necessity that boards of education act within the limits of the Bill of Rights.

That they are educating the young for citizenship is reason for scrupulous protection of Constitutional freedoms of the individual, if we are not to strangle the free mind at its source and teach youth to discount important principles of our government as mere platitudes.[70]

In *Wieman v. Updegraff*,[71] which held an Oklahoma loyalty oath unconstitutional, Justice Frankfurter concurring asserted:

That our democracy ultimately rests on public opinion is a platitude of speech but not a commonplace in action. Public opinion is the ultimate reliance of our society only if it be disciplined and responsible. It can be disciplined and responsible only if habits of open-mindedness and of critical inquiry are acquired in the formative years of our citizens. The process of education has naturally enough been the basis of hope for the perdurance of our democracy on the part of all our great leaders, from Thomas Jefferson onwards.[72]

Barnette, in Justice Jackson's broad formulation, concerned the unconstitutionality of involuntary affirmation of belief. *Wieman,* like *Keyishian v. Board of Regents*,[73] (quoted in *Tinker*) involved the First Amendment rights of teachers. The *Tinker* Court extended the passive *Barnette* right to remain silent to the active right to speak. It converted the *Keyishian* right of the teacher to initiate a "robust exchange of ideas"[74] into the student right to do the same.

Tinker is also the culmination of a line of cases which no longer accept shaping a uniform national character as a legitimate educational purpose. Justice Fortas cites *Meyer v. Nebraska*[75] as confirmation of "this Nation's repudia-

[69] West Virginia State Board of Education v. Barnette, 319 U.S. 624, 635 S. Ct. 1178 (1943).
[70] *Ibid.,* 1185.
[71] Wieman v. Updegraff, 344 U.S. 183, 73 S. Ct. 215 (1952).
[72] *Ibid.,* 344 U.S., 196.
[73] *Supra,* n. 68.
[74] Keyishian v. Board of Regents, *op. cit.*
[75] Meyer v. Nebraska, 262 U. S. 390, 43 S. Ct. 625 (1923).

tion of the principle that a State might so conduct its schools as to 'foster a homogeneous people.' "[76] In *Meyer* the Court struck down a Nebraska statute which prohibited, *inter alia,* teaching foreign languages to pupils below the eighth grade. The statute sought to insure that children of foreign-born parents would learn the English language and American ideals without competition from another tongue taught in the schoolroom. The Court held that application of the statute to a foreign language teacher in a private school violated the substantive due process rights of the teacher to follow his calling and of the parents to engage him to instruct their children in the language. The Court noted, however, that its decision did not apply to the state's power to prescribe the curriculum in public schools. While Justice McReynold's opinion in *Meyer* rejected the unity theme of American educational history, its language, transferred to the new context of the *Tinker* case, is even more striking. Justice McReynolds repudiated use of the schools to foster homogeneity of language and culture. *Tinker* is aimed at the far more subtle and comprehensive effort on the part of some schools to achieve homogeneity of ideas. In this respect it is closer to Justice Jackson's opinion in *Barnette*.

The theme of Justice Jackson's opinion is that in the toleration of diversity lies our national strength.

To enforce those rights today is not to choose weak government over strong government. It is only to adhere as a means of strength to individual freedom of mind in preference to officially disciplined uniformity for which history indicates a disappointing and disastrous end.[77]

While Justice Jackson notes that national unity as a goal which officials may foster by persuasion is not in question, history teaches that use of coercion to achieve uniformity will ineluctably lead to tragedy. "Compulsory unification of opinion achieves only the unanimity of the graveyard."[78] We must, then, reject this course and realize that

We can have intellectual individualism and the rich cultural diversities that we owe to exceptional minds only at the price of occasional eccentricity and abnormal attitudes.[79]

A number of contemporary lower courts also seem to have picked up, at least

[76] Tinker v. Des Moines Independent School District, *op. cit.,* 739.
[77] 63 S. Ct. at 1185.
[78] *Ibid.,* 1187.
[79] *Ibid.,* 1187.

in the area of dress, the *Barnette* perception that the purpose of education has moved away from uniformity and adjustment to diversity and independence. What was a surprising opinion even as a dissent in *Pugsley v. Sellmeyer*[80] is increasingly becoming the majority view. For instance, in *Westley v. Rossi*[81] the school authorities had contended, *inter alia,* that the school "must assume its share of responsibility for seeing to it that students dress neatly and appropriately and that they develop habits of cleanliness and good grooming."[82] The court responded:

The rule is an attempt to impose taste or preference as a standard. The standards of appearance and dress of last year are not those of today nor will they be those of tomorrow. Regulation of conduct by school authorities must bear a reasonable basis to the ordinary conduct of the school curriculum or to carrying out the responsibility of the school. No moral or social ill consequences will result to other students due to the presence or absence of long hair nor should it have any bearing on the wearer or other students to learn or to be taught.[83]

A parallel comment is made by Judge Watson in the Superior Court decision in *Myers v. Arcata Union High School District*[84]:

The limits within which regulations can be made by the school are that there be some reasonable connection to school matters, deportment, discipline, etc., or to the health and safety of the students. . . . The Court has too high a regard for the school system . . . to think that they are aiming at uniformity or blind conformity as a means of achieving their state goal in educating for responsible citizenship. . . . Certainly, the school would be the first to concede that in a society as advanced as that in which we live there is room for many personal preferences and great care should be exercised insuring that what are mere personal preferences of one are not forced upon another for mere convenience since absolute uniformity among our citizens should be our last desire.[85]

In *Richards v. Thurston*[86] Judge Wyzanski distinguished the general high school from a military academy where, arguably, uniformity may be justified.

But in schools of general comprehensiveness the constitutional premise is that "from

[80] *Supra,* p. 7.
[81] Westley v. Rossi, 305 F. Supp. 706 (D.C. Minn. 1969).
[82] *Ibid.,* 710.
[83] *Ibid.,* 713-714.
[84] Myers v. Arcata Union High School District, Unreported decision, quoted in ACLU, *Academic Freedom in the Secondary Schools, rev'd* 75 Cal. Rptr. 68 (Ct. of App. 1969).
[85] *Ibid.,* 19.
[86] Richards v. Thurston, 304 F. Supp. 449 (D.C. Mass. 1969).

different tones come the best tune." Heraclitus. [citation omitted] They illustrate our national motto E PLURIBUS UNUM.[87]

In the district court opinion in *Breen v. Kahl*[88] the court responded to the traditional argument of the school authorities that long hair distracts other students from their work by asking:

Is it a desirable objective of our public schools to eliminate diversity within the school in order to eliminate distraction? On the contrary, is it not more vital to encourage experience with diversity and adaptation to it, in a diverse nation and world, than to encourage homogeneity?[89]

The court in *Zucker v. Panitz*,[90] a non-haircut case, reflects the same approval of diversity and, in addition, controversy. Here the principal of the school prevented the editors of the student newspaper from publishing in the paper a paid advertisement in opposition to the Vietnam war. The school administration argued, *inter alia,* that the advertisement contravened a school policy which limited the contents of the paper to school news and prohibited advertising which expressed a point of view on any subject not related to the high school. The administrators testified that the policy was necessary to preserve the journal as an educational device. The court noted in response:

If the Huguenot Herald's contents were truly as flaccid as the defendants' argument implies, it would indeed be a sterile publication. Furthermore, its function as an educational device surely could not be served if such were the content of the paper.[91]

Tinker, like the above cases, might be a response, or at least an antidote, to the quest for uniformity critics assert our schools are engaged in. According to these observers American schools chiefly prize attitudes of acquiescence and submissiveness in students. Hence students are taught that disagreement is disobedience. The *Tinker* case strikes at the core of this development. It is an attempt to separate out for protection the elements of freedom to disagree from the imperatives of school discipline.

In order for the State in the person of school officials to justify prohibition of a particular expression of opinion, it must be able to show that its action was caused by something

---

[87] *Ibid.,* 453.
[88] Breen v. Kahl, 296 F. Supp. 702 (W.D. Wis. 1969), *aff'd,* 83 U.S.L.W. 2332 (7th Cir. 1969).
[89] *Ibid.,* 709.
[90] Zucker v. Panitz, 299 F. Supp. 102 (S.D. N.Y. 1969).
[91] *Ibid.,* 103.

more than a mere desire to avoid the discomfort and unpleasantness that always accompany an unpopular viewpoint.[92] . . . Clearly, the prohibition of expression of one particular opinion, at least without evidence that it is necessary to avoid material and substantial interference with school work or discipline, is not constitutionally permissible.[93]

Post-*Tinker*: Possibilities and Prospects

Because of the vagueness of the formula "substantial interference with school work or discipline," it is problematical how successful the Court's efforts to separate speech from discipline will turn out to be. The terms "school work" and "discipline" remain to be defined in later cases. Moreover, the factual situation in *Tinker* is of little precedential value. While the Court was reluctant to label the armbands as "pure speech," the unobtrusiveness of the demonstration was fairly clear.[94]

The possibilities for emasculation of the *Tinker* holding lie first in the traditional willingness of courts to define broadly "interference with discipline" in cases dealing with student criticism of school policy and personnel.

In the *Dresser* case,[95] for example, the court said expulsion was proper since the satirical poem tended to "set at naught the proper discipline of the school, impair the authority of the teachers, and bring them into ridicule and contempt."[96]

In *Lander v. Seaver*[97] a student was walking by the teacher's house after school and called him "Old Jack Seaver" in the presence of other students. The teacher overheard and whipped the offender in school the next day. The court denied the student's suit for damages since the remark had "a direct and immediate tendency to injure the school, to subvert the master's authority, and to beget disorder and insubordination."[98]

In *Wooster v. Sunderland*[99] the student, in an address to the student body, declared certain rooms in the building fire hazards, denounced the school board

[92] Tinker v. Des Moines Independent School District, *op. cit.*, 738.
[93] *Ibid.*, 738-739.
[94] Henkin, The Supreme Court, 1967 Term Foreword: On Drawing Lines, 82 Harv. L. Rev. 63, 76-82 (1968).
[95] See p. 10 *supra*.
[96] State ex. rel. Dresser v. District Board, *op. cit.*, 116 N.W., 235.
[97] Lander v. Seaver, 32 Vt. 114 (1859).
[98] *Ibid.*, 120.
[99] Wooster v. Sunderland, 27 Cal. App. 51, 148 p. 959 (1915).

for compelling the student body to hold its meetings and social events in an auditorium with inadequate fire exits, and criticized the board for prohibiting various hazing activities in the school. The court, citing *Dresser,* upheld the expulsion of the student on the ground that

The admitted purpose of the plaintiff's address was to belittle the defendants [school board members] in their official capacity; and the whole tenor of the address was well calculated to produce not only that result, but to engender as well, in the minds of the students, a feeling of disrespect for the defendants, and a secret if not open hostility to their control of the student body and management of school affairs. Such being the natural tenor and tendency of the plaintiff's address, his conduct in making the same cannot be classed as anything but a species of insubordination to constituted authority, which required correction at the hands of the defendants in order that the discipline of the school might be maintained.[100]

In *Wilson v. Abilene Independent School District*[101] the court upheld an anti-fraternity regulation, quoting with approval a Corpus Juris statement that a school board can prohibit fraternities "where it is shown that such societies have a tendency to destroy good order, discipline, and scholarship, and such a tendency is sufficiently shown by fraternity publications containing articles written in a spirit of insubordination to the school authorities."[102]

A departure from this line of thought is *Murphy v. Board of Directors of Marengo District.*[103] During a school board inspection of the school a local political journal published two articles written by a student and critical of the board. The court overturned the board's expulsion of the student, because the disciplinary statute invoked by the board referred only to dismissal "for gross immorality, or for persistent violation of the regulations of the school," and not to the specific out-of-school actions of the expelled student. If it wanted to, however, the court could have invoked "the common law of the school" to fill the gaps in the disciplinary statute relied upon by the board. This was the technique used by the court in *Dresser,* which relied upon "certain obligations on the part of the pupil, which are inherent in any proper school system . . . and which may be enforced without the adoption in advance of any rules upon the subject."[104]

[100] *Ibid.,* 961.
[101] Wilson v. Abilene Independent School District, 190 S.W. 2d 406 (Tex. Ct. of App. 1945).
[102] *Ibid.,* 190 S.W. 2d at 410.
[103] Murphy v. Board of Directors of Marengo District, 30 Iowa 429 (1870).
[104] State ex. rel. Dresser v. District Board, 116 N.W. 233.

The responses of contemporary courts which have dealt with the school have varied. In *Norton v. East Tennessee State University Discipline Committee*[105] students distributed a pamphlet which criticized campus apathy and compared it unfavorably to the activity on other campuses where students had seized buildings. The pamphlet urged students to "stand up and fight" and referred to the university administration as "despots." The Sixth Circuit Court of Appeals upheld the suspension of the students on the ground that the pamphlet was an "open exhortation to the students to engage in disorderly and destructive activity."[106] The court said it would be difficult to maintain discipline on the campus if this type of activity was permitted. In *Tinker,* the court pointed out, "the children did not urge a riot, nor were they disrespectful to the teachers."[107] The court also asserted that whereas in *Tinker* there were no facts that would reasonably have led to an expectation of substantial disruption of school activities, here the dean and the president did foresee such disturbances.

Jones v. State Board of Education,[108] another college case, is significant for the opinion on the district court level. Here three college students were expelled for "disruptive conduct." Two of the students had committed literally disruptive acts, such as breaking up a student-faculty meeting. The third, Jones, distributed literature advocating a student boycott of fall registration. Nevertheless, the court concluded that expulsion was justified for all three since their actions had "promoted unrest and disrupted the normal educational activities of the University."[109]

On appeal the Sixth Circuit affirmed,[110] stating that the record revealed numerous acts not entitled to constitutional protection. The various offenses by the court duplicated those mentioned by the district court, except for the cryptic addition that Jones had lied at the hearings before the disciplinary committee. It is not clear whether the court relied on Jones' misconduct at the hearing to affirm the lower court decision. The Supreme Court clearly did, denying certiorari since Jones had also been suspended for lying at the suspension hearing.[111]

[105] Norton v. East Tennessee State University Discipline Committee, 419 F. 2d 195 (6th Cir. 1969), *cert. denied,* 38 U.S.L.W. 3506 (U.S. June 22, 1970) (No. 1011).
[106] *Ibid.,* 198.
[107] *Ibid.,* 199.
[108] Jones v. Board of Education, 279 F. Supp. 190 (M.D. Tenn. 1968), aff'd, 407 F. 2d 864 (6th Cir. 1969), *cert. denied,* 396 U.S. 817, 90 S. Ct. 145.
[109] *Ibid.,* 279 F. Supp. at 190.
[110] *Ibid.,* 407 F. 2d 836 (6th Cir. 1969).
[111] *Ibid.,* 90 S. Ct. at 145.

These cases point up a central dilemma of the *Tinker* formula: the type of speech most important to students—that directed at the schools they attend—is the type some courts seem most willing to characterize as interfering with the discipline or the work of the school. These courts view "interference with school work or discipline" in the manner of the *Dresser* court, thereby including in that phrase speech critical of school rules or disrespectful of school personnel. *Norton* and *Jones* demonstrate, moreover, the willingness of some courts to proscribe as potentially disruptive speech which in the adult world would merely be considered highly polemical. Judge Celebrezze in *Norton* dissented to this approach. Pointing out the standard of incitement to lawless action recently set up by the Supreme Court in *Brandenburg v. Ohio*,[112] he urged that courts require that school authorities show incitement—and a likelihood of disruption resulting—rather than mere advocacy in order to justify curtailment of speech.[113] Justice Marshall, dissenting to the Supreme Court's denial of certiorari, agreed, pointing out that "On this record, there was nothing approaching incitement of the kind which could constitutionally be punished as extending beyond the realm of speech into that of action."[114] Under the *Tinker* test school authorities must be able to produce facts which would reasonably lead them to forecast substantial disruption of school activities.[115] Incorporating the *Brandenburg* test into this formula, only action which is directed to inciting and is likely to incite would amount to a reasonable "forecast" in situations such as those in *Norton* and *Jones*. This combined test would also effectively quiet the ghost of "Old Jack Seaver" of the *Lander* case[116]; merely "disrespectful" speech would have no greater significance than it enjoys in the adult world.

In addition, the history of *Scoville v. Board of Education*[117] suggests that a court should not be able to restrict student speech critical of school rules merely by the device of labeling it inciting on its face. In the *Scoville* case the plaintiffs distributed a student literary journal which included an editorial urging the student body to refuse to accept or to destroy upon acceptance "all propaganda that Central's administration publishes." The editorial also called attendance regulations "utterly idiotic," said the dean had a "sick mind," and concluded that "our whole system of education with all its arbitrary rules and schedules seems

---

[112] Brandenburg v. Ohio, 395 U.S. 441, 89 S. Ct. 1827 (1969).
[113] 419 F. 2d at 208-209.
[114] 38 U.S.L.W. at 3507.
[115] Tinker v. Des Moines Independent School District, *op. cit.*, 89 S. Ct. at 740.
[116] *Supra*, p. 586.
[117] Scoville v. Board of Education, 286 F. Supp. 988 (N.D. Ill. 1968), *aff'd.*, 415 F. 2d 860.

dedicated to nothing but wasting time."[118] The plaintiffs were expelled and sought mandamus.

The district court assumed as true plaintiffs' allegation that the distribution of the magazine created no disturbance. Nevertheless the court concluded that the content of the speech made it an immediate incitement to disregard of administrative regulations necessary to orderly maintenance of the school system and thus interfered with the special public use to which the property had been dedicated.

On appeal, however, the Seventh Circuit Court of Appeals, sitting *en banc*, reversed the district court and remanded for further factual inquiry, noting that criticism of school rules did not per se justify the expulsions. Rather, the lower court should have examined the impact of the publication, the ages of the persons to whom it was sold, and other circumstances surrounding its distribution in an effort to determine whether the publication could have in fact reasonably led the school board to forecast substantial disruption.

Courts averse to the incorporation of *Brandenburg* into the *Tinker* doctrine might attempt to make use of the loophole opened up by the district court in *Scoville*. Perhaps sensing the weakness of its characterization of the speech as inciting, the court here sought reinforcement by pointing out that the speech was directed to "an audience which, because of its immaturity, is more likely than an adult audience to react to the detriment of the school system."[119]

An appropriate rejoinder to the *Scoville* attitude might be found in the *Norton* dissent where Judge Celebrezze pointed out that the pamphlets were not distributed among an angry group, "but on a campus of presumably tempered and rational students."[120] Of course, it is uncertain whether courts will be willing to apply this language to secondary school students. In *Schwartz v. Schuker*[121] a student was suspended for distributing an underground newspaper on school grounds in violation of the principal's order. The court stressed with respect to the distribution:

A special note should be taken that the activities of high school students do not always fall within the same category as the conduct of college students, the former being in a

[118] 286 F. Supp. at 989.
[119] 286 F. Supp. at 992.
[120] Schwartz v. Schuker, 38 U.S.L.W. at 2318.
[121] 298 F. Supp. 238 (E.D. New York 1969).

much more adolescent and immature stage of life and less able to screen fact from propaganda.[122]

A second problem of the *Tinker* formula is its invitation to the courts to apply to the school situation a variation of what Kalven calls the "Heckler's Veto."[123] The classic Heckler's Veto problem involves a speaker whose words, while not inciting to the impartial observer, irritates to the point of violence an especially sensitive or already hostile crowd. The question the Court has grappled with is whether the police may arrest the speaker for breach of the peace rather than protecting his right to speak by arresting unruly members of the crowd.

The inclination of some courts to prohibit the speech rather than protect the speaker in school situations is brought out most clearly in the recent spate of high school grooming cases. The reason usually given by school authorities and courts for grooming regulations is that long hair often leads to distraction of other students, or attacks on long-haired students with consequent disruption of the educational process. The distracted or attacking students, in other words, are the hecklers.

The grooming cases follow similar patterns. The school principal will appear in court to testify in general to the problems of distraction and disturbance which accompany long-haired males in the schools. Sometimes he will relate specific examples which have occurred in the school. Courts will respond within a broad range of factual and constitutional conclusions. Some courts will deny long hair the status of a constitutional right and therefore uphold the grooming rule on a minimal showing of distraction.[124] Other courts will consider long hair a First Amendment or *Griswold v. Connecticut*-type personal right and demand a strong showing of distraction or disturbance, which usually cannot be met by the school.[125] A final group of courts will grant long hair constitutional status but find that the school authorities have met their burden of proving distraction and disruption and therefore should prevail.[126] It is this

---

[122] 419 F. 2d at 208.

[123] Kalven, *The Negro and the First Amendment*, 140-141 (1965).

[124] Leonard v. School Committee, 349 Mass. 704, 212 N.E. 2nd 468 (1965).

[125] Breen v. Kahl, 83 U.S.L.W. 2332 (7th Cir. 1969); Griffin v. Tatum, 300 F. Supp. 60 (M.D. Ala. 1969); Richards v. Thurston, 304 F. Supp. 449 (D.C. Mass. 1969).

[126] Ferrell v. Dallas Independent School Dist., 392 F. 2d. 697 (5th Cir. 1968), *cert. denied*, 393 U.S. 924; Crews v. Cloncs, 303 F. Supp. 1370 (S.D. Ind. 1969); Akin v. Board of Education, 68 Cal. Rptr. 557 (Ct. of App. 1968).

group that gives the hecklers their veto and therefore presents the gravest implications for free speech in the schools.

The conflict between distraction and free speech is dramatized in the majority and dissenting appellate opinions in the *Ferrell* case.[127] Here the principal had testified at the trial to a number of disruptive incidents related to long hair: a group of boys had tried to trim the hair of a long-haired schoolmate; some boys had picked fights with long-haired students; girls had come to his office to complain about obscene remarks directed at long-haired boys. The court concluded that the grooming rule was of compelling necessity to the orderly operation of the school.

That which so interferes or hinders the state in providing the best education possible for its people, must be eliminated or circumscribed as needed. This is true even when that which is condemned is the exercise of a constitutionality protected right.[128]

Judge Tuttle's dissent stated the opposite view. Noting that courts seemed too willing to cut off the free speech privileges of dissenters because of fear of disorder or even violent reaction by supporters of the status quo, he asserted:

It seems to me it cannot be said too often that the constitutional rights of an individual cannot be denied him because his exercise of them would produce violent reaction by those who would deprive him of the very rights he seeks to assert.[129]

Under *Tinker,* we have noted, school authorities may proscribe speech if facts exist which would reasonably lead them "to forecast substantial disruption of, or material interference with, school activities."[130] While *Tinker* extends First Amendment rights to students, this limiting formula might be used by schools to nullify the substance of these rights. The formula is pitched towards preservation of the status quo. No matter how rationally articulated or softly-spoken, the more unorthodox an opinion is the more susceptible it is to disruptive response. The *Tinker* test is phrased in terms of the quality of the audience, not the quality of the speech. A militantly conservative student body can veto the speech of a vocal radical and vice-versa.

On the other hand, it should be recognized that the fact that the speech, no matter how sober and calm, occurs in a school does present certain imperatives

---

[127] *Supra* n. 126.
[128] 392 F. 2d at 703.
[129] *Ibid.*, 705.
[130] Tinker v. Des Moines Independent School District, *op. cit.*, 740.

lacking in the outside-school situation. A violent reaction to a speaker in a public auditorium or park will usually result only in disruption of the speech. The same reaction in a school disrupts not only the speaker, but whatever school work is going on at the same time. Hence, unswerving support of the free speech privileges of the speaker in school is not a realistic position.

The weakness of the *Tinker* formula lies in its generality. There is no explicit requirement that school authorities who reasonably anticipate substantial disruption take affirmative steps to remove the threat beyond merely curtailing the speech. In his dissent in *Ferrell* Judge Tuttle points out that the suspended students had not themselves disturbed the peace; rather, they were barred because of the anticipated reaction of their classmates. It is the actions of the latter, he concludes, that should be prohibited, not the expressions of individuality of the suspended students.[131] Judge Tuttle's approach suggests that school authorities can diminish the possibilities of disruption by issuing firm warnings to those who would disrupt rather than by opting for the more convenient technique of prohibiting the speech. Courts should consider reading this suggestion into the *Tinker* formula. A forecast of substantial disruption would not then be "reasonable" unless the school authorities had first made a concerted effort to discourage disrupters.

The limits of this requirement are brought out in *Guzick v. Drebus*.[132] Here a student was suspended for wearing an anti-Vietnam button in violation of a no-button rule in the high school. According to the opinion, the rule was instituted against a background of severe racial strife in the Cleveland high schools. The school administrators described the school as a racial tinderbox and testified that they established the rule because many of the buttons were racially provocative. The court upheld the rule on the ground that under the *Tinker* formula the wearing of buttons presented a threat of substantial disruption. The court argued that it would be impossible to administer a rule which prohibited only racially-provocative buttons. The administrative difficulties seem rather contrived, however, in light of the New York Board of Education's recent resolution on "Rights and Responsibilities for Senior High School Students" prohibiting distribution of material advocating racial or religious prejudice.[133]

---

[131] Ferrell v. Dallas Independent School District, *op. cit.*, 392 F. 2d at 706.
[132] Guzick v. Rebus, 305 F. Supp. 472 (N.D. Ohio 1969).
[133] *N.Y. Times*, Oct. 30, 1969, p. 37.

The court is, however, expressing legitimate concern in prohibiting racially-oriented buttons. It is fairly certain that regulations and threats aimed at those who might attack the wearer of such buttons are sure to fail. In this situation the heckler's veto incorporated into the New York resolution seems justified. Absent the special racial situation, however, courts should examine scrupulously the potentialities for disruption asserted by school authorities and demand an effort on their part to lessen such potentialities without curtailing the speech.

An additional feature of the *Guzick* case is the reappearance of the traditional education-for-unity argument in the totally new setting of racial tension. The court contended that the buttons tended to foster division among the student body and magnify differences between students. This old view of education as a means of creating uniformity seems unrealistically sanguine against the background of Black-White strife emphasized by the court. Clearly the differences between the students will not be blurred by removing buttons since the persons who wear them, unlike the immigrants of pre-World War I days, want the differences to remain. Even more important to our analysis, the wearers and many others would vigorously dispute the court's contention that eliminating differences among students is any business of the schools.[134] It seems likely that the homogeneity educational purpose, used to support button bans, anti-fraternity regulations, and haircut rules, will finally succumb to attacks by prideful blacks asserting the right to organize all-black students associations and wear Afros and dashikis.

The *Guzick* case, as one of the first judicial manifestations of the intersection of free speech and racial conflict in the schools, also tells us something about where educational purpose is going. For most of our history education was likened to a chemical change: students were viewed as inert elements easily moulded by an educational system political in its goals. Behind the alarmed tone of the judge in *Guzick* is the realization that the periodic table of American education has turned. Students, suddenly volatile, are no longer willing to be acted upon. They are, in the words of the Supreme Court in *Tinker*, "persons."[135] If, as *Tinker* and many of the grooming cases suggest, uniformity, compliance, and uncritical patriotism are moribund themes in American education, it might

[134] The New York High School Student Union has asked for the creation of clubs along ethnic lines with funds from the school General Organization. Wasserman & Reimann, "Student Rebels vs. School Defenders: A Partisan Account," 4 Urban Review 9, 13 (Oct. 1969).
[135] Tinker v. Des Moines Independent School District, *op. cit.*, 739.

be because the schools have no choice. Uniformity and compliance cannot be achieved where there is active resistance. While courts might attempt to whittle down to the size of impetuous children the persons created by *Tinker,* it is clear the big change has already occurred: students have become active determinants of educational purpose both in law and in fact.

Title I of ESEA:
The Politics of Implementing
Federal Education Reform*

JEROME T. MURPHY

Harvard University

Most of the literature on Title I of ESEA focuses either on activities at the federal level—the passage and early administration of the law—or at the local level—the quality of programs or alleged abuses in using Title I funds. Little attention has been paid to the intergovernmental problems of implementing education reform in a federal system. In this article, the author examines the interaction between the different levels of government concerning Title I, focusing mainly on the program's management and on specific federal efforts to issue strong guidelines. The discussion reveals the political and bureaucratic obstacles which constrain federal efforts to redirect local priorities and explores the notion of countervailing local power as a way for the poor to gain greater leverage in the program's operation.

If there was a single theme characterizing the diverse elements of the 1965 Elementary and Secondary Education Act (ESEA), it was that of reform. The Act

* A substantially different version of this article appears in *Inequality in Education* (No. 6) published by the Harvard Center for Law and Education.

The author wishes to express his appreciation to Robert Binswanger, Samuel Halperin, Walter McCann, Michael Olneck, Joel Sirkin, and particularly David Cohen, for their critical reading of earlier drafts and their helpful suggestions.

Harvard Educational Review Vol. 41 No. 1 February 1971, 35-63

was designed to stimulate innovation, to strengthen the states, to link research with the schools, and to make the problems of the poor the nation's number one education priority. In short, ESEA was the first step toward a new face for American education. Almost six years after passage it is worth asking whether this spirit of reform has been translated into educational practice. Has state and local administration reflected these new priorities? Has the U.S. Office of Education (USOE) asserted leadership? What are the political and bureaucratic impediments to reform? How can implementation be improved?

Answers to these questions are important for two reasons. First, they will provide useful information about the limits of federally-initiated reform. After all, the extent to which states and localities meet the new priorities is a measure of the balance of power within the federal system as well as of the central government's capacity to execute reform. Second, a better understanding of the problems of implementation can lead to improvement in ESEA's operation. That understanding can best be achieved, I believe, by viewing key administrators at the federal, state, and local level as primarily political figures—rather than educators—subject to the demands of their constituencies and to the constraints of their bureaucracies.

To answer these questions, I have focused on Title I, aid to the disadvantaged. This program, the heart of ESEA, provides a good test of the limits of federal reform. It is the largest program by far and called for the greatest change at the local level—a new focus on the needs of the poor. This paper, then, examines the origins of Title I, the nature of the agencies administering it, and the working relationships between one state department of education (Massachusetts), the USOE, and local school districts. Finally, it describes some recent efforts to make the program more responsive to the program's clients, the poor.[1]

Federal Legislation for the Disadvantaged

The central thrust of ESEA is to eliminate poverty. The underlying notion was familiar—poor children given the opportunity to do well in school will do well

---

[1] A variety of means were used to gather the information for this study. Interviews were conducted in the USOE, in the Massachusetts Department of Education and at the local level. Other information was gathered through reports, Congressional hearings, questionnaires, correspondence, conversations, memoranda, and, of course, a reading of the general literature. In addition, some of the material is based on my personal experence with the program, gained while working for the Department of Health, Education, and Welfare between 1964 and 1969.

as adults—and it was embodied in the Act's first and most important Title. By allocating extra funds to schools with high concentrations of poor families, federal reformers sought better education and improved opportunity.

In this, Title I expressed the political atmosphere prevailing in mid-'60's Washington. The Economic Opportunity Act of 1964 had just been passed, and high government officials believed that poverty soon would be eliminated. It was only natural, then, that they would try to extend the President's "unconditional war" on poverty by providing quality education for poor children. This attitude also reflected the influence of what Daniel P. Moynihan calls the professionalization of reform:

[President Kennedy's] election brought to Washington as officeholders, or consultants, or just friends, a striking echelon of persons whose profession might justifiably be described as knowing what ails societies and whose art is to get treatment underway before the patient is especially aware of anything noteworthy taking place. . . .[2]

This predisposition was translated into law in the 1965 ESEA, mainly through the work of Commissioner of Education Francis Keppel, a strong advocate of concentrating resources on disadvantaged children. He was aided by a bill (S.2528), introduced by Senator Morse (D-Oregon) in 1964, which suggested a formula for concentrating funds on cities and rural areas at the same time, thus helping to assure a coalition of northern urban and southern rural Congressmen. Through negotiations with key individuals and interest groups, the details of ESEA were hammered out prior to the bill's introduction, successfully avoiding major amendments during Congressional debate.[3]

It is important to understand that the reform was not a response to public pressure. Unlike the great national programs passed during the New Deal, Title I did not arise from public demand. The poor were unorganized and had made no demands for such legislation. Nor was Title I a natural outgrowth of tried and tested programs at the local level. At the time it was developed, only three states (California, Massachusetts, and New York)[4] had passed legislation specifically

[2] Daniel P. Moynihan, *Maximum Feasible Misunderstanding* (New York: The Free Press, 1969), p. 23.

[3] See Stephen K. Bailey and Edith K. Mosher, *ESEA: The Office of Education Administers a Law* (Syracuse: Syracuse University Press, 1968); Philip Meranto, *The Politics of Federal Aid to Education in 1965* (Syracuse: Syracuse University Press, 1967); James W. Guthrie, *The 1965 ESEA: The National Politics of Educational Reform* (Unpublished Ph.D. dissertation, Stanford University, 1967).

[4] *Title I/Year II, the Second Annual Report of Title I of the Elementary and Secondary Education Act of 1965, School Year 1966-67* (U. S. Office of Education, 1968), pp. 119-121.

geared to disadvantaged children, and those laws funded only small pilot projects. Other local efforts were new, few, and concentrated in a limited number of cities.[5] Nor was Title I the creature of the established educational organizations or educational administrators. The "old guard" bureaucracy in USOE viewed its job as providing technical assistance to the states and local schools when requested. They saw USOE more as a consulting firm than a focal point for leadership or initiative; the guiding principle was deference to the states and the local schools, and they had reservations about Title I.[6] The attitude of the professionals who staff the state and local school systems was little different. They were "dismayed" to learn that ESEA was not general aid,[7] and in a national survey of school administrators in May, 1966 approximately 70 percent stated that Title I funds should not be allocated on the basis of poverty.[8] As far as the educational associations in Washington were concerned, their primary interest was general support for ongoing public school activities.[9] Although they accepted the poverty theme as a necessary compromise to achieve aid for the public school system, their emphasis was on breaking barriers to federal aid, on the ground that this would be a major step toward general support at a later date. As one observer put it:

Having passed the Senate seven times and the House twice since the 1960's, a large-scale school aid measure had yet to reach the President's desk for signature.... 'Getting the law on the books' was the objective uniting perhaps the widest constellation of interest groups ever assembled on a domestic issue.[10]

In sum, Title I was not a reflection of pressure from the poor and had little support among educational administrators. Some urban school officials saw the need for categorical aid, but most support from within the profession was based on the notion that Title I was the first step toward general aid. The objective was a law, not reform. The main thrust for aid to poverty schools came from reformers in the Executive Branch who had a double objective: the establishment of the principle of federal aid to schools and a redirection of local priorities.

[5] See statement by Francis Keppel, U. S. Commissioner of Education, *Hearings Before the General Subcommittee on Education, on Aid to Elementary and Secondary Education,* 89th Congress, First Session, House, p. 89.
[6] Bailey and Mosher, *op. cit.,* p. 47.
[7] *Ibid.,* p. 99.
[8] *Ibid.,* p. 306.
[9] *Ibid.,* pp. 15, 16.
[10] Samuel Halperin, "ESEA: Five Years Later," unpublished paper printed in the Congressional Record, September 9, 1970, p. H8492.

The Allocation of Responsibility

The successful implementation of reform depends heavily on the distribution of power. Given USOE's historically weak role in American education, the reformers saw the need for additional federal leverage. The legislative record, however, was mixed on this point. While the reformers were anxious to use federal power to improve schooling for the poor, they were acutely aware of their limitations. Federal control of schools was a major issue when the bill was drafted, and every increment in federal power meant a corresponding decrease in the states' authority.

The result was a complicated and highly significant compromise. The formula-grant mechanism was used to by-pass the states and localities in determining roughly on whom the money should be spent. Funds were to be distributed among school districts based on the relative incidence of poverty, and within each school district they would be spent on educationally deprived (not necessarily poor) children in areas of high concentration of poverty.[11] The poverty formula is simply a device to get the money to those geographic areas of greatest need based on the premise that there is a high correlation between poverty and educational deprivation. The formula grant system cuts both ways, however; while it by-passes state and local governments, it establishes a virtual entitlement for each state and locality, once the total amount of federal appropriation is known. This absence of competition for program funding combined with the local view that the money is rightfully theirs immensely weakens the ability of federal officials to bargain with the states over improvements in administration.[12]

Initiative as to program content and character was left with the states and localities. The local school districts identify eligible educationally deprived children, determine their needs, design programs to meet them, and apply to the appropriate state department of education for approval. The state departments approve projects of sufficient "size, scope, and quality," monitor them, and sub-

[11] My discussion of Title I is limited to programs administered at the local level by the public schools. Title I also provides support for the handicapped, for institutionally neglected or delinquent children, for Indian children, and children of migrants.

[12] This comment is not meant as a criticism of the Title I formula. When it was being developed in the fall of 1964, a major concern was a politically acceptable way to distribute funds. The formula met this criterion since funds were concentrated in key Congressional districts in urban areas and poor rural sections of the South. Also the formula allowed the Administration to come up with estimates, prior to Congressional action, showing each Congressman how much his district would receive if the proposal passed. The formula's effect on bargaining during implementation may be viewed as an unanticipated consequence.

mit fiscal reports and evaluations of the effectiveness of the local projects to USOE. The federal role in this respect was minimal—it consisted of little more than approving applications submitted by the state departments of education for participation in the program. This application is simply a two-page letter signed by a state official stating, in effect, that the law will be followed.

The only counterweight to this almost complete delegation of programmatic responsibility was an effort to reserve federal authority to establish "basic criteria," which could be used to guide administration of Title I at the state and local level. Although this provision in the draft legislation emerged unchanged from the Congress, it caused considerable controversy in both houses.[13] It was viewed as a threat to local control of the schools and was hotly contested during Congressional debate. The resistance portended future obstacles to the exercise of the federal quality control authority.

In summary, Title I provides influence for each level of government, but at the same time sets limits. The USOE by-passes the state departments of education in determining the allocation of grants and establishes basic criteria which must be met by local districts, but it has no operating control over the projects. The states have the responsibility for approving projects but they must apply federal criteria in carrying out this responsibility. Local districts have access to earmarked funds and latitude in designing projects, circumscribed only by the effectiveness of state supervision and federal criteria. Thus, even on paper, the local school districts had the greatest say in how Title I funds were to be spent. Other factors, discussed below, also tend to favor local interests over state and federal.

The Administration of Title I: Federal Efforts

It is beyond the scope of this paper to describe in detail the administration of Title I by USOE. The initial problems of reorganizing the agency, of recruiting "new blood," of staffing the programs, and of writing the regulations and guidelines have been amply and adequately covered by Bailey and Mosher in their book, *ESEA: The Office of Education Administers a Law*.[14] Some observations, however, are in order.

After nearly 100 years of efforts to obtain general federal support for ele-

---

[13] See *Hearings before the General Subcommittee on Education, op. cit.,* p. 176; *Report No. 146,* 89th Congress, First Session, Senate, p. 84.
[14] Bailey and Mosher, *op. cit.*

mentary and secondary schools, it is not surprising that passage of ESEA was viewed as a tremendous breakthrough. The much tougher job, however, was to implement the reform. But the problem of administrative niceties was not the focus of the reformers. As former U.S. Commissioner of Education Harold Howe explains:

ESEA was the only type of Federal activity in education which was likely to be political-ly viable in 1965. . . . I doubt that anyone could have dreamed up a series of education programs more difficult to administer and less likely to avoid problems in the course of their administration, but ESEA was not designed with that in mind.[15]

Also, the reformers involved in the development and passage of ESEA for the most part were not involved in its implementation. They went on to the development and passage of additional legislation, while federal administration of ESEA was turned over to lower levels in the 98-year-old USOE. This staff had virtually no impact on the development of Title I, and would have preferred more traditional approaches or general aid. The agency had no experience with grants-in-aid of the size and scope of Title I, nor had it ever been called on to write "basic criteria" governing the approval of projects. Herculean efforts were made to bring in new blood and make the agency responsive to its new and different responsibility, and the agency did change. Nevertheless, the "old guard," if not always controlling policy, were the ones who for the most part staffed the program and made the day-to-day decisions setting the tone of the federal operations.

Furthermore, USOE has not had enough people to effectively monitor the program. Title I is administered by the Division of Compensatory Education in the Bureau of Elementary and Secondary Education of the USOE. Monitoring is carried out by area desk officers in the Operations Branch. Although Title I policy is usually set at higher levels, the area desk officers are the link with the states and have day-to-day responsibility to assure that the states are following the law, regulations, guidelines, and basic criteria.

While as recently as January, 1970, there were some thirty professionals working on all facets of Title I—technical assistance, accounting, program support— there were only three area desk officers for the entire nation.[16] The one[17] dealing

---

[15] Letter from Harold Howe II, September 18, 1970.

[16] In the early days of the program, the Division of Program Operations (later the Division of Compensatory Education) approached its authorized personnel strength of 82 (including professional and clerical staff) (Bailey and Mosher, *op. cit.*, p. 93) but subsequently dwindled.

[17] Interview with Benjamin Rice, Midwest and Eastern Regional Representative, Division of Compensatory Education, USOE.

with Massachusetts had responsibility for twenty-three other states, the District of Columbia, Puerto Rico, and the Virgin Islands. In addition to his Title I responsibilities, he spent approximately two-thirds of his time working on other projects at the Bureau level having practically nothing to do with Title I. The desk officer had no assistants and spent a substantial part of his Title I time drafting replies to Congressional mail. He felt that he could use at least four assistants to provide adequate technical assistance to the states.

In addition, the USOE staff has traditionally taken a passive role with respect to the states. The Massachusetts desk officer described his relationship with the Massachusetts Title I Director as "very nice." In the six months preceding the interview, they had met together once and talked occasionally on the telephone. The area desk officer viewed his job as one of trouble-shooting, answering complaints, and providing service. He did not want to provide leadership, nor did he view himself as a program "monitor" in the sense of being an enforcement officer. He readily admitted that he did not have the time to know what was going on in his states, and thus was dependent on information supplied by state officials as to whether they were enforcing the law. He found the limited staff situation frustrating, not because he was unable to monitor the states, but because he could not give them assistance.

The prevailing *modus operandi* was succinctly described by an official in the Division of Compensatory Education who has been with the program since its start:

Title I is a service-oriented program with predetermined amounts for the states. This sets the framework where the states are entitled to the money. Other than making sure states got their money and making sure it was spent, there was no role for the Office of Education. I don't know anyone around here who wants to monitor. The Office of Education is not investigation-oriented, never has been, and never will be.

During the last few months, however, the Title I staff has grown significantly. As of October, 1970 there were some fifty professionals, including fifteen new desk officers, on the Title I staff.[18] While this increase gives the appearance of greater control of the program, it is too early to assess its full impact at the state and local level. It seems fairly clear, though, that USOE's service-oriented attitude toward the states has not changed significantly. After all, changing the style of a bureaucracy rooted in tradition cannot be accomplished overnight. Further-

---

[18] Estimates supplied by Holly Knox, Office of Legislation, USOE.

more, as one USOE official commented: "Most of the new people are state-oriented."[19]

But why the sudden jump in staff size? The underlying cause can be traced to the fall of 1969 and the release of the report, *Title I of ESEA: Is It Helping Poor Children?* The so-called Martin-McClure Report (named after its authors Ruby Martin of the Washington Research Project and Phyllis McClure of the NAACP Legal Defense and Educational Fund, Inc.) charged flagrant violations of the law. USOE responded with a high level Title I task force. This focus of attention on an obviously understaffed program combined with continuing pressure from the report's authors led to the increase in staff.

But the report's importance goes far beyond its identification of problems; its release may well mark a turning point in the administration of Title I. The report represents the first major effort by spokesmen of the poor to bring significant pressure to bear on USOE.[20] Later in the paper we shall see that a growing new Title I constituency, largely triggered by the report, has also had some impact on Title I guidelines and is tenaciously tugging at the established powers in education.

The area desk operation is not the only respect in which federal administration of Title I has been weak. Since the beginning of the program, evaluation has been high on the list of federal rhetorical priorities, but low on the list of actual USOE priorities. The reasons for this are many. They include fear of upsetting the federal-state balance, recognition of that little expertise exists at the state and local levels to evaluate a broad-scale reform program, and fear of disclosing failure. No administrator is anxious to show that his program is not working.

The matter is further complicated by the lack of agreement on what would prove whether Title I is "working." This confusion stems from covert disagreements over the relative importance of Title I's several purposes. These include breaking the federal aid barrier, raising achievement, pacifying the ghettos, building bridges to private schools, and providing fiscal relief to school districts. Depending on one's perspective and priorities, Title I may be or may not be working. If one views the program primarily as a vehicle to provide fiscal relief for a city school system, achievement test scores are hardly an appropriate way to measure success; the program is successful if fiscal collapse is avoided. The legislation, however, calls for objective measures, and if they show that children are not

[19] Interview with Terry Lynch, area desk officer, Division of Compensatory Education, USOE.
[20] For a description of events leading to the report, see pp. v, vi of the report.

gaining in achievement it makes it difficult for Congressmen to justify their continued support of the program. At the same time, it is politically dangerous to be opposed to program evaluation. Therefore, inconclusive evaluations are politically acceptable, although they may provoke rhetorical wrath in the Congress, and exasperation in the Executive agencies.

Another important area of federal responsibility involves the federal audit reviews. These are conducted by the HEW Audit Agency, and their purpose is to determine whether funds are being spent in accordance with the legislation, regulations, and guidelines. These reviews are fairly comprehensive—in fact, they are the only full-scale investigations of Title I operations at the state and local level which HEW undertakes. Since 1965, audits have been conducted in twenty-four states and the District of Columbia; two have been conducted in Massachusetts.[21] The results are always referred to the Division of Compensatory Education for action. According to the Martin-McClure study of Title I:

The audit reports have brought to light numerous violations of the law and have recommended that millions of dollars be recovered by the Federal government. Yet in only three cases has the Office of Education sought and received restitution of funds illegally spent. . . . Even in the most flagrant cases of unlawful use of the money—the two swimming pools in Louisiana for example—the Office of Education has failed to act.[22]

The fundamental question is why has USOE not been more aggressive in managing the program and following up on the audits. Limited staff and a service orientation are only part of the answer. There are several other interrelated factors which help to explain USOE's attitude. First, in the early days there was pressure to get the program moving quickly and to get federal-state relations off on the right foot. There was a natural tendency to overlook alleged misuses and accentuate the positive. Second, there was tremendous pressure on program administrators to generate statistics on the number of schools involved, the number of children affected, and so forth, so that the Administration could demonstrate the program's success to the public and the Congress. Third, there was fear that if USOE pushed too hard the Congress would replace categorical programs with general aid, in which case USOE would have even less influence.

---

[21] *Title I of ESEA. Is It Helping Poor Children?* A report by the Washington Research Project of the Southern Center for Studies in Public Policy and the NAACP Legal Defense and Educational Fund, Inc., 1969, p. 52. The first audit in Massachusetts covers the first year of operation, 1965-66, the second covers 1966-68.

[22] *Ibid.*, pp. 52, 53.

Another factor is that it is one thing to try to persuade a state to follow certain criteria, but an altogether different thing to accuse it of misusing funds which it views as its money. While Congressmen abhor waste and never tire of abusing bureaucrats who countenance waste, these are general principles which do not necessarily apply to individual cases, particularly if alleged misuses occur in their own districts. Top federal officials recognize the political nature of their jobs and know that they need Congressional support to survive. Thus, they are not anxious to arouse Congressional wrath—especially when there is a high probability that they will not get the money back. USOE staff remembers well the Presidential veto in October, 1965 of Commissioner Keppel's attempt to cut off funds from Chicago for civil rights violations.[23] The basic problem, then, is political, and Morton Grodzins describes the situation neatly:

The undisciplined [political] party system impels administrators to seek political support for their programs. The parties do not supply this support, and administrators and their programs cannot survive without it . . . [This situation makes] the administrator play a political role.[24]

Finally, USOE's behavior has in part been adapted to take advantage of its strategically weak bargaining position. It is virtually impossible for USOE to cut off funds which the states view as their rightful entitlement under the law. The states know this and so does USOE; thus, orders or demands by USOE are bound to be ineffective since they cannot be backed up with action. Furthermore, demands might alienate the states and result in loss of communication. Since USOE's influence comes mostly from the power of persuasion and since it is presently almost totally reliant on the states for information about local programs, it is absolutely essential that USOE maintain cordial relations with the states. Under these bargaining conditions, the states are in a position to exact a price for their good will. As a result, USOE will be willing to sanction (perhaps covertly) deviations from the statute in exchange for open communications. Thus, the agency's service orientation and deference to local officials can be understood in part as rational behavior, designed to achieve the greatest possible influence from a weak bargaining position. USOE's problem, then, is not simply the lack of will or lack of staff, but lack of political muscle. And like other politi-

[23] Bailey and Mosher, *op. cit.*, pp. 151, 152.
[24] Morton Grodzins, *The American System: A New View of Government in the United States* (Chicago: Rand McNally and Company, 1966), p. 270.

cians, many key federal administrators are unwilling to take risks unless pressured.

There are some examples, however, where the USOE has attempted to assert leadership. For the most part these efforts have been unsuccessful. This is best exemplified in USOE's attempts to establish two basic criteria—one calling for the establishment of local parent advisory councils and the other governing the concentration of funds. Since the beginning of the program, USOE has sought to involve parents in local Title I programs on the theory that the more parents were involved the better their children would do in school. In general, however, USOE has been unable to enforce this notion on the states. In 1969, three out of five school districts did not have Title I local parent advisory councils.[25]

The first set of basic criteria was issued by the USOE on April 14, 1967 responding to what the memorandum described as a "definite need"[26] for states to apply specific criteria in approving local projects. It called for parent participation in Title I programs, but was not specific on the nature of this participation other than to say that it should be "appropriate."[27] The second set of basic criteria (issued on March 18, 1968) went a step further. It called for the involvement of parents "in the early stages of program planning and in discussions concerning the needs of children in the various eligible attendance areas."[28] Four months later (July 2, 1968), the USOE issued a separate memorandum focusing on community and parent involvement calling for the establishment of a formal mechanism for their involvement. The memorandum stated that

each Title I applicant *must* have an appropriate organizational arrangement. This means, in effect, that *local advisory committees will need to be established* for the planning, operation, and appraisal of a comprehensive compensatory educational program.[29] (Emphasis added.)

This aroused considerable concern. It was one thing to discuss parent involvement, but quite another to call for formal committees which could be identified,

[25] David S. Brown and Edward E. Rosendahl, "A Summary of Findings Extracted from the Preliminary Report Entitled, Education of the Disadvantaged, Fiscal Year 1969." Bureau of Elementary and Secondary Education, USOE, July, 1970, p. 19.

[26] Memorandum from John F. Hughes, Director, Division of Compensatory Education, USOE, to Chief State School Officers, April 14, 1967, p. 1.

[27] *Ibid.*, p. 7.

[28] Memorandum from Commissioner Harold Howe II, USOE, to Chief State School Officers, March 18, 1968, p. 4.

[29] Memorandum from Commissioner Harold Howe II, USOE, to Chief State School Officers, July 2, 1968, p. 1.

counted, and perhaps exert some influence over the program's direction. Many educators viewed these committees as a threat to professional control.

Seventeen days later, under pressure from interest groups, local educators, and the Congress, a clarifying memorandum was sent to the Chief State School Officers, retreating from the previous position. The new memorandum stated:

> In most instances it will be advantageous for a local educational agency to establish a local advisory committee. . . . In some instances, however, local conditions may favor other arrangements. . . . Whatever arrangement is decided upon, it should be one which your office, in the light of its understanding of the local situation, finds likely to be effective. . . .[30]

In effect, USOE told the states to do as they pleased. When asked about the status of local advisory committees in Massachusetts, the USOE area desk officer for Massachusetts stated: "Frankly, I've heard nothing about them. Haven't heard any complaints."

In frustration over the apparent lack of implementation of local advisory committees, the Division of Compensatory Education convinced the Nixon Administration to recommend that local advisory committees for Title I be explicitly included in the law.[31] The recommendation was made and the provision added by the House Committee on Education and Labor. It was dropped, however, during floor debate by the House of Representatives on the 1969 amendments to ESEA because of strong opposition, particularly from Southern Congressmen. The bill that emerged from the Congress (April 13, 1970) further confused the matter with unclear language on the extent of USOE's authority.[32]

During the following six months, USOE once again worked to devise a guideline covering local parent advisory councils. At one point a draft was circulated requiring parent councils for each Title I project area. Representatives of the public school lobby met with USOE officials and flatly asserted that requiring councils was unacceptable. Unlike the past, however, USOE was also under pressure from the other side. Groups coordinated by the Washington Research Project were pushing USOE to promulgate strong requirements. As a spokesman for the National Education Association stated: "USOE has been getting pressure from

---

[30] Memorandum from Commissioner Harold Howe II, USOE, to Chief State School Officers, July 19, 1968, p. 1.

[31] Most important decisions made by USOE are the products of bargaining among persons holding different points of view. The decision to push for legislation was not an exception to this general rule.

[32] See Section 415 of Title IV of Public Law 90-247 as amended by Public Law 91-230.

some groups I've never heard of. I don't know whether they represent a constituency or not." Finally on October 30, 1970, a compromise emerged from USOE requiring "system-wide" parent councils.[33]

This guideline represents a small but significant victory for groups representing the poor. After all, it is not very often that the public school lobby is forced to compromise, particularly on a matter related to the control of the public schools. But the story may not be over yet. It remains to be seen whether the requirement survives Congressional scrutiny.

A similar pattern exists in federal efforts to require concentration of funds. One of the critical issues addressed in the original draft guidelines was the concentration of limited resources for a limited number of students. USOE officials believed that if Title I was to have any impact, the money could not be spread thin. The original provision in the draft guidelines (Fall, 1965) stated that the number of children served could be no greater than the number of children in the district counted under the poverty formula. This effort to concentrate funds met with strong disapproval from both the Congress and professional interest groups who argued that the standard was not consistent with Congressional intent. Strong opposition also was expressed about other provisions of the guidelines and regulations. In November, 1965, the word came down from Commissioner Keppel to "slenderize" the documents.[34] The concentration provision was removed from the guidelines. This defeat set the stage for the determination of future standards.

USOE's first set of basic criteria (April 14, 1967) proposed twelve criteria and included "a supporting statement of the types of evidence or indications that the applicant's proposal should contain in order to show that it meets the criterion."[35] The criterion regarding concentration simply stated: "Title I services will be programmed so that the services provided will be concentrated on a limited number of children."[36] The supporting discussion, however, established a new standard:

The investment per child on an annual basis for a program of compensatory educational services which supplement the child's regular school activities should be expected to equal

[33] Memorandum from T. H. Bell, Acting U. S. Commissioner of Education, USOE, to Chief State School Officers, October 30, 1970, p. 2.

[34] Interview with John F. Hughes, former Director of the Division of Compensatory Education, USOE. He stated that Commissioner Keppel was under political pressure to cut back on the guidelines.

[35] Memorandum of April 14, 1967, *op. cit.*, p. 1.

[36] *Ibid.*, p. 4.

about one-half the expenditure per child from State and local funds for the applicant's regular school program.[37]

Exactly ten days later, under Congressional pressure, the USOE issued a "clarifying" memorandum, retreating from the thrust of the original memorandum. It read in part:

The criteria statements are the requirements to be met, whereas the discussion matter *provides guidance* in meeting the criteria. It should be expected, of course, that the discussion guides *may not be fully applicable to every project application.*[38] (Emphasis added.)

Under the terms of the "clarifying" memorandum, then, the new concentration standard provided only "guidance" and was not "fully applicable to every project application." Thus, within ten days the new standard had been rendered impotent.

Not satisfied that funds were being adequately concentrated, USOE issued another memorandum on November 20, 1968 focused specifically on improving the quality of Title I. The draft memorandum that went to Commissioner Howe's desk for signature specifically called for the implementation of the concentration standard by 1970. At the last minute, under political pressure, the draft was pulled back by the USOE Bureau of Elementary and Secondary Education and revised.[39] The concentration standard was replaced by the hastily drawn statement: "Plan the program so that by 1970 the average Title I expenditure per child in high priority areas is *raised to a significant level.*"[40] (Emphasis added.) Nowhere in the memorandum is "significant level" discussed or defined and nowhere is the previous standard mentioned. Thus, a memorandum which had begun in the Division of Compensatory Education as an attempt to accomplish greater concentration of resources emerged from the bureaucracy with no standard even as "guidance." Meanwhile, dollar expenditures per Title I child have been decreasing each year, and 30% of the students participating in 1968 were not disadvantaged while millions of eligible students went unaided.[41]

[37] *Ibid.*, p. 4.

[38] Memorandum from John F. Hughes, Director of Compensatory Education, USOE, to Chief State School Officers, April 24, 1967, p. 1.

[39] According to John F. Hughes, *op. cit.*

[40] Memorandum from Commissioner Harold Howe II, USOE, to Chief State School Officers, November 20, 1968, p. 2.

[41] *Education of the Disadvantaged, an Evaluative Report on Title I Elementary and Secondary Education Act of 1965,* fiscal year 1968, USOE, 1970, p. 97.

This chronology of federal efforts to establish strong basic criteria points to USOE's weakness in influencing local priorities. Time after time local and state educators, mainly through Congressional intervention, were able to have their priorities recognized in federal directives, diluting federal attempts to gain leverage. But local pressure is not limited to efforts to prevent USOE from asserting leadership. It also is used to initiate federal guidelines backing up local priorities. This allows local and state authorities to "pass the buck" and claim that they are constrained by federal directives, when in fact federal action is a result of local pressure. This can be seen clearly in a recent controversy surrounding the use of Title I funds for clothing.

Last summer, the National Welfare Rights Organization, with the encouragement of the Washington Research Project, started a drive to increase Title I expenditures for clothing. The organizers saw the effort as a way for parents to gain greater political control over the program. The first incident took place in Providence, Rhode Island, with welfare mothers reportedly demanding a clothing allowance of $48 per Title I child.[42] To neutralize this pressure, the Rhode Island Title I coordinator urged the USOE to promulgate a strong guideline restricting Title I expenditures for clothing. USOE complied with a guideline on August 14, 1970 setting forth numerous requirements.[43] During the next few weeks, however, similar pressure for clothing grew in New York City, Cleveland, Ohio, and Norfolk, Virginia.[44] As a result, USOE was pressured by Chief State School Officers, school superintendents, and state Title I coordinators to come out with even more stringent guidelines. USOE officials were sympathetic to the schoolmen's concern; they viewed the demands of the welfare mothers as a threat to Title I's "integrity" and the whole operation as a "raiding party." On September 15, 1970 a new guideline stated that Title I is "an educational program, not a welfare program" and that funds could be used for clothing "only in emergency situations."[45] Furthermore, the guideline prohibited "any increase over previous years" in the proportion of local Title I expenditures for clothing. Enraged by what they viewed as repressive and illegal restrictions, representatives of the National Welfare Rights

[42] "Education U.S.A., Washington Monitor," National School Public Relations Association, September 28, 1970, p. 24.
[43] Memorandum from Thomas J. Burns, Acting Associate Commissioner for Elementary and Secondary Education, USOE, to Chief State School Officers, August 14, 1970.
[44] "Education U.S.A., Washington Monitor," *op. cit.*, p. 24.
[45] Memorandum from T. H. Bell, Acting U. S. Commissioner of Education, USOE, to Chief State School Officers, September 15, 1970, p. 1.

Organization and the Washington Research Project met with Secretary of Health, Education, and Welfare Richardson. Shortly thereafter, on October 5, 1970, a third guideline on clothing was issued which repealed the ceiling on clothing expenditures.[46] Nevertheless, the other restrictions in the previous two guidelines were confirmed.

The merits of the clothing demands are not at issue here. What is important for my discussion is the fact that schoolmen apparently were able to get USOE to issue immediately strong guidelines reflecting local priorities. By contrast, it is interesting to note that the flagrant violations of Title I alleged in the Martin-McClure Report evidently were not viewed as a threat to the program's integrity, although they were viewed as a serious problem. The response was the establishment of a Task Force which a year later has yet to issue its report. No doubt changes will result—I have pointed out some—but the different responses to the clothing issues and the Martin-McClure Report simply reflect the obvious—USOE is mainly responsive to its major constituency, the public school system. Nevertheless, the clothing episode also demonstrates that counter-pressure can have some impact on USOE, in this case through pressure brought to bear on the Secretary of Health, Education, and Welfare.

These descriptions of guidelines and of program management illustrate the context in which USOE officials operate. They are indisposed to compliance activities to begin with, but even if this were not the case, the staff to operate an effective compliance program has not existed. Furthermore, even if both the staff and the will were present, they lack the political support to assert leadership. Most federal legislators are sure to be more responsive to the wishes of state and local school officials than to the desires of bureaucrats in the Executive Branch. As a result, the Title I program administrators act as though their main constituency lies in the Congress and the state and local school officials, rather than among the poor people whose children the legislation is supposed to assist. Only recently are there some signs that this is changing. But as long as these counter-pressures—in the Congress and at the state and local level—remain relatively weak, federal officials will be almost powerless to enforce their standards on state and local school systems. Either they will not try to enforce federal standards, or their efforts at enforcement will be continually challenged and frustrated.

[46] Memorandum from T. H. Bell, Acting U. S. Commissioner of Education, USOE, to Chief State School Officers, October 5, 1970.

The Administration of Title I: State Efforts

The problems, of course, do not lie only within the USOE, or between it and the Congress. There are important barriers to implementing the legislative priorities at the state level, and in the relations between federal, state, and local school government. These problems appear in Massachusett's efforts to monitor the program and in the state's response to federal initiatives.

One important problem lies in the fact that many state departments of education provide little educational leadership, and Massachusetts has been no exception. In 1965, a report characterized its Department as "a conglomerate historical institution trying earnestly and valiantly to become an organization."[47] Following the recommendations of this report, the legislature the same year passed a bill calling for a major overhaul of the Department, reorganizing it into five manageable divisions. Five years later, however, a follow-up study found:

The Department of Education, for many reasons, continues to carry out a wide variety of mandated functions, most of which have little to do with educational leadership or which have any visible impact on improving quality of education for students in our schools.[48]

In part this is a problem of personnel. For one thing, it is extremely difficult for the Department to staff its activities; in January, 1970 there were 70 professional positions funded but vacant.[49] Low salaries are a major reason for this difficulty. The remuneration for professionals in the Department is simply not competitive with that for other educators in the state with comparable credentials. But even apart from this, the staff is not varied in background, training, or experience. A 1969 study found a striking degree of homogeneity in the backgrounds and career patterns of the top officials in the Massachusetts Department. For example, the eight who responded to the study questionnaire all had prior experience as teachers and school administrators, and none was born, raised or had been a teacher or administrator in a city with a population of more than 100,000.[50] Homogeneity, of course, is not the same as incompetence. It may tend,

[47] Report of the Special Commission Established to Make an Investigation and Study Relative to Improving and Extending Educational Facilities in the Commonwealth. Commonwealth of Massachusetts, House Document No. 4300, June 1965, p. 130.

[48] John S. Gibson, *The Massachusetts Department of Education: Proposals for Progress in the 70's. Final Report.* Tufts University, September 1970, p. 95.

[49] *Ibid.*, p. 130.

[50] James A. Buckley, *A Study of the Professional Staffs of the New England State Departments of Education.* Unpublished special qualifying paper, Harvard Graduate School of Education, 1969, pp. 20-24.

however, to establish an inbred, insular attitude and approach which probably are resistant to new ideas, innovation or acceptance of employees from different backgrounds.

These personnel problems carry over into the state's Title I unit of five professionals. Of the four responding to my questionnaire on their careers, all had past experience as teachers, and three of the four worked as school administrators. All were white. Although the state Title I director[51] has been unsuccessfully trying to hire two additional staff members, his problem is not money. For several years the state has been returning federal funds earmarked for state administration of the program; almost $100,000 was returned in 1969.[52] The Title I director argues that a major problem is finding competent people willing to work for the Department.

A second problem is staff size. Even if the two new professionals were added, this would leave seven people to monitor some 420 projects, with a total cost of $16 million.[53] Furthermore, the Title I unit is responsible for state management of seven other federal programs related to the disadvantaged.[54] Considering this work load, it would appear impossible to even visit each Title I project once a year, let alone understand what is being done with the money.

The third problem is that the state Title I staff is not oriented toward compliance activities. They view themselves as professional educators, and the idea of enforcement or regulation is simply incompatible with their view of public education. The state Title I director views his job as providing technical assistance and service, and he strives for cordial and cooperative relationships with local school districts. When they employ questionable practices, he tries to discourage them through friendly persuasion. In effect, the Title I director expresses the same reluctance to interfere with local prerogatives that federal officials express about interfering with state prerogatives. Moreover, he sees his role vis-a-vis local districts—technical assistance and service—the same way that his federal counterparts perceive their role toward Massachusetts. To paraphrase one student of federalism,[55] what usually happens is that federal, state, and local educators, work-

[51] Interviews with Robert L. Jeffrey, Senior Supervisor in Education and Massachusetts Department of Education Title I Director.

[52] Daniel C. Jordan and Kathryn Spiess, *Compensatory Education in Massachusetts: An Evaluation with Recommendations*, School of Education, University of Massachusetts, March 1970, p. 12.

[53] Estimates provided by Robert L. Jeffrey, *op. cit.*

[54] Jordan and Spiess, *op. cit.*, p. 344.

[55] Daniel J. Elazar, *American Federalism: A View from the States* (New York: Thomas Y. Crowell Company, 1966), p. 149.

ing in the same program, trained in the same schools, and active in the same professional associations, think along the same lines and have relatively little trouble in reaching a meeting of minds.

These personnel problems, of course, have an enormous impact on Massachusetts' management of Title I. This is evidenced in the state's efforts to monitor Title I, mainly through meetings with local educators, project audits, and program evaluation. Much of the state Title I office staff time is spent in consultation with local Title I coordinators. In fact, a good part of the approval process is handled informally through telephone conversations and visits to the state office prior to the submission of formal applications. This is supplemented by visits to local projects, with emphasis placed on those districts receiving more than $100,000 a year under Title I. Recently, task forces have been set up to visit the six largest cities. In addition to the visits, regional conferences and workshops are held to discuss matters of mutual concern to Title I coordinators. These visits, conversations, and conferences, however, are very time-consuming and provide virtually no opportunity for a limited staff to see whether the Title I funds are spent in accordance with the law.

The Department's financial management procedures are even weaker. The second HEW audit report on Massachusetts concluded that "significant improvements in procedures and practices are needed at both the State and local levels. . . ."[56] The audit found that for the fiscal years 1966, 1967, and 1968 the Department allowed Title I allotments of more than $1 million to lapse each year because of ineffective management.[57]

The situation in Boston dramatizes the problem:

Even though the amount of $263,000 was unused by the City of Boston in fiscal year 1968, we found that certain eligible attendance areas with high concentrations of children from low-income families in the City of Boston were receiving minimal services for meeting the special educational needs of these children. . . . We were advised by City of Boston program directors that the limited availability of funds precluded them from providing additional services in these areas.[58]

Although three auditors are paid with Title I funds, only one actually audits local projects. The others do some bookkeeping for the program but also spend

---

[56] HEW Audit Agency, *Report on Review of Grants Awarded to the Commonwealth of Massachusetts Under Title I, Elementary and Secondary Education Act of 1965.* January 23, 1969, p. 3.
[57] *Ibid.,* p. 4.
[58] *Ibid.,* p. 20.

much of their time on non-Title I activities. The Title I director states that the Department is developing a team approach for auditing all federal programs although no date has yet been set for implementation. The second HEW audit report states:

We found that (1) the SEA [State Department] does not have any written procedures, audit guidelines, and/or audit standards for conducting audits, ... (2) no audits of LEA's [local districts], however inadequate, were performed on any fiscal year 1968 projects; and less than one-third of fiscal year 1967 projects at LEA's were reviewed as of November, 1968....[59]

The only audit report local districts are required to submit is a one-page sheet which breaks down Title I expenditures by educational categories such as instruction, food, administration, and divides the expenditure into salaries, contracted services, and other expenses. It is absolutely useless in efforts to determine whether funds were spent in accordance with the law.

The HEW auditors examined four school districts in depth. They found inadequate time and attendance records, lack of substantiation of overtime pay to teachers, inadequate accounting procedures covering contractual services, inadequate equipment controls and unremitted unused funds. One school district was found with inaccurate financial reporting.[60] The Title I coordinator of this school district stated that he knew about the audit discrepancies because he met with the auditors before they left the school system. He said, however, that he had never heard from the State Department about correcting the matter.

The State Title I director does not believe that money is being misused in Massachusetts but admits that he has no way of proving this. He would like to have more auditors for Title I but again argues that it is difficult to get competent people to work for the Department.

A similar pattern exists in the state's execution of its responsibilities for program evaluation. Title I requires local districts to make annual evaluation reports to the states, including "appropriate objective measurements of educational achievement."[61] Unlike previous federal programs, this provision called for the public display and disclosure of information which schoolmen knew could be used against them in the enforcement of new priorities. The evaluation provisions also put strain on the many local school districts and state departments of

[59] *Ibid.*, p. 5.
[60] *Ibid.*, p. 6.
[61] 20 U.S.C. 241e.

education which had little evaluation experience. It is no wonder that from the start there has been reluctance and resistance toward fully implementing this provision of Title I, and a tendency toward obfuscation. After all, to the extent that evaluations do not disclose meaningful information on program results, local districts can meet their own priorities without being subject to challenge based on evidence of failure.[62]

Evaluation activities in Massachusetts have produced very little useful data. According to Cohen and Van Geel:

The analysis in the [Massachusetts Title I] state [evaluation] report is meaningless, then, because the data it collected could serve no conceivable evaluative purpose. Collecting this information was, in the strict sense of the word, futile. . . .[63]

The approach of the Massachusetts Department to local districts on this point corresponds to the federal approach to the states: little direction. This is apparent from a recent internal memorandum. Referring to fiscal year 1971, the Title I director's office states: *"Next year, all projects will be expected to show evidence of evaluation and to indicate how the evaluation contributes to modifications in project activities."*[64] (Emphasis added.) Apparent frustration with Massachusetts' commitment to Title I evaluation is also expressed in the memorandum:

If we are serious about obtaining meaningful information about the impact of these projects and these funds and about fostering continued improvement in Title I, we must

[62] As an example of the type of local evaluation reports the state receives from participating districts, I analyzed the fiscal year 1968 annual report of the public schools for one community in the Metropolitan Boston area. The school system's evaluation of its reading program concludes that the overall effect of Title I has been a positive one, citing the fact that fourth-grade Title I children went from 5 months behind non-Title I children in September, 1967 to 4 months behind in June, 1968 on a standardized reading test. Examination of the supporting data indicate that the gap did close. The report, however, failed to point out the reason: the non-Title I group regressed 2 months in reading during the year, while the Title I group fell back only one month. Although the net result may be a closing of the gap, these data hardly support the conclusion of positive benefits under Title I.

During the 1968 fiscal year, the Department had only two full-time staff supervisors, plus three part-time specialists to cover all phases of some 460 separate Title I projects. Discrepancies and inaccuracies like the one above simply could not be picked up. Thus, we find school districts with the natural desire, as well as the political necessity, to show the success of their program, and virtually no follow-up analysis by the Department of the data submitted to them.

[63] David K. Cohen and Tyll van Geel, "Public Education" in *The State and the Poor,* ed. by Samuel H. Beer and Richard E. Barringer (Cambridge: Winthrop Publishers, 1970), p. 231.

[64] Memorandum prepared in Jeffrey's office at the request of the Director of the Division of Elementary and Secondary Education, December, 1969, p. 11.

devote substantial effort to the immediate and long-range approaches that state and local communities take in the area of productive and useful evaluation.[65] (Emphasis added.)

There are signs, however, after years of virtual inaction, that the Department is attempting to improve the situation. Consultants have been hired and the Title I director would like an evaluation expert for his permanent staff. In addition, conferences were held last spring announcing the state's intention to require evidence of success or progress before a project can be refunded. Some of the motivation for this strong stand, no doubt, came from the release in March 1970 of a comprehensive study of Title I, sponsored by the Massachusetts Advisory Council on Education.[66] The study found that less than half of the local projects sampled had an evaluation design and two of every three made little or no effort to analyze their evaluation data.[67] Despite the conferences and the report, the Title I director admitted that no projects were turned down this year because of failure to show success. Furthermore, apparently none of the study's recommendations has yet been carried out and the Department is now in the process of choosing an outside group to make recommendations on the study's recommendations. Prospects for improvement remain gloomy. Cohen and Van Geel conclude:

At a minimum, improving the state department's evaluation capacity would add between $150,000 and $200,000 a year to the budget. And supporting the experiments required for effective research and development (assuming no reallocation of funds within the Title 1 budget) would require a huge increase in that budget. If state education revenues are the sole source, neither step will be easy to arrange.[68]

This description of Massachusetts' management of Title I highlights the devastating impact of personnel problems on all phases of monitoring—state-local consultation, project auditing, and program evaluation. But major obstacles to implementing the federally-initiated reform would remain even if the Massachusetts Department hired additional competent staff. The reasons for this are basically political. In the federal system, states have no inherent reason for following federal directives, such as basic criteria, unless they are rewarded or penalized for their action. Since states receive their full entitlement for mere participation in Title I—as opposed to producing some specified result, or doing a good job—there are virtually no reasons to follow federal directives. State officials know

[65] *Ibid.,* p. 12.
[66] Jordan and Spiess, *op. cit.*
[67] *Ibid.,* p. 28.
[68] Cohen and van Geel, *op. cit.,* p. 234.

that there would not be any major repercussions for ignoring federal directives, even with USOE's knowledge. As we saw earlier with the HEW audits, USOE has been quite reluctant to take any action even when the purported violations were blatant. In fact, not only are incentives missing, but federal efforts to persuade the states to follow the federal directives have been almost nonexistent. The Massachusetts Department for the most part does not hear from USOE except for occasional memoranda, and USOE is looked upon mainly as a consultant. The Massachusetts Title I director states: "USOE provides technical and administrative assistance. They are helpful. . . . They won't come out flatly and say what you can't do. I don't feel any kind of control. It just isn't there." As an example, last spring USOE sent a team to Massachusetts to review the state management of the program. The Title I director described the visit as "helpful" but half a year later the Department is still in the process of examining USOE's recommendations. Furthermore, the Title I director stated that the recent increase in the USOE Title I staff has not yet resulted in any new pressure from Washington. Thus, Massachusetts is fairly free to ignore federal directives conflicting with state priorities. The state Title I director passes the federal memoranda on to the local districts if he thinks they are "significant," but the Department does not take them (or the audit reports) too seriously. For example, it took Massachusetts nine months to respond to the second HEW audit report. The Title I director attributed the delay to "bureaucratic lag." This casual attitude, however, is not without grounds; USOE, a year later, has still not replied to Massachusetts.[69] The matter remains unresolved.

Another illustration is evidenced in Massachusetts' response to the previously discussed federal efforts to concentrate resources on a limited number of children. Although sympathetic to the idea of concentration, the Department disagreed with the standard contained in the original basic criteria and simply did not enforce it. The final memorandum—dropping the standard—was passed on to the local districts.[70] One local district's Title I coordinator stated that he had never been encouraged to concentrate Title I resources on fewer children until the summer of 1969, and, as far as he knew, no standard was ever adopted by Massachusetts. In the summer of 1970, however, the Department issued a memorandum calling for $200 per Title I child.[71] Nevertheless, new project applications falling below this standard continue to be approved by the state.

[69] According to Robert L. Jeffrey, *op. cit.*
[70] *Ibid.*
[71] Memorandum from Lawrence M. Bongiovanni, Director, Bureau of Elementary and Secondary Education, Massachusetts Department of Education, to Superintendents of Schools and Title I, ESEA, Directors, June 26, 1970, p. 3.

When state priorities are consistent with federal priorities, on the other hand, the states can use the federal priorities to back up their efforts to influence local policy. The Massachusetts Department happened to favor the establishment of local advisory councils, and therefore welcomed the federal criterion of July 2, 1968 requiring them. To encourage implementation at the local level, the Department distributed the memorandum to all participating school districts. The July 19, 1968 USOE memorandum, which weakened the requirement, was not distributed.[72] Thus, the Department was in a position to push its own priority by arguing with local districts that the reason to establish local advisory committees was the federal pressure, when in fact the USOE had already retreated from that position. Despite Massachusetts' urging, more than half of the Title I projects in 1969 did not have parent councils.[73]

This reliance on a federal criterion to support a state priority reflects in part the historical balance of power between state and local prerogatives in Massachusetts. This balance can be further illustrated by one recent example. In 1969 the Department sent a memorandum to the Boston Public Schools regarding program modification which previously had been discussed with local officials. In the directive the Department stated that Boston "must" rather than "should" make certain modifications. The matter was brought to higher levels and was resolved by the staff of the Massachusetts Chief State School Officer and the staff of the Superintendent of Boston Public Schools: "must" was changed to "should."

Just as USOE is unable to dictate to the states, similarly the Massachusetts Department is in general unable to impose state priorities on local districts. Part of the explanation lies in the historical commitment in Massachusetts to local control of the schools and the resultant concentration of power at the local level. The Title I director characterized local control as " 'The Battle Hymn of the Republic' of New England educators." But part of the explanation, as noted earlier, stems from the formula grant system. The absence of competition for Title I funds weakens the state's bargaining position as it does USOE's. Districts receive fixed amounts almost regardless of their programs. Few applications for funds have ever been rejected, and funds have never been withheld. Because of these political factors and its serious personnel problem, the Massachusetts Department is deprived of its leverage to control local expenditures. As a result, even when federal priorities are consistent with state priorities, implementation depends on

[72] According to Robert L. Jeffrey, *op. cit.*
[73] Jordan and Spiess, *op. cit.*, p. 43.

local priorities which often may be different. A recent study of Title I evaluation in Boston points out the conflict:

Looking back over this period of five years since Title I evaluation was brought to Boston, we can see there has been a clear absorption of all federal and state attempts (especially state attempts) to improve the quality of the evaluation . . . not only has the federal thrust toward reform been absorbed by the school system, it has been turned to the advantage of Boston to serve Boston's own needs.[74]

Conclusion

This discussion of bureaucracy and politics reveals some of the pitfalls in implementing federally-initiated reform and suggests the present limited capacity of federal and state agencies to carry through the hoped-for reform. Translating an Act into action is marked by marginal changes, not sudden great leaps forward.

Whose priorities are being met, then?

The answer is that local schools are fairly free to meet their own priorities. Local autonomy is respected by the Massachusetts Department of Education, and state persuasion is no more effective on important decisions affecting local programs than is federal pressure on the state. That is not to say that the local school districts blatantly violate the law, only that they are in control of the situation and are able to stretch the law to meet the needs of their constituencies which include more than the poor. The Department and USOE exercise little effective direction and have only superficial knowledge of how the money is being spent.

Why has Title I been administered in this way?

To blame the problems on timidity, incompetence, or "selling out" is to beg the question. I have identified a number of contributing causes: the reformers were not the implementers; inadequate staff; a disinclination to monitor; a law and tradition favoring local control; and absence of pressure from the poor. The primary cause, however, is political. The federal system—with its dispersion of power and control—not only permits but encourages the evasion and dilution of federal reform, making it nearly impossible for the federal administrator to impose program priorities; those not diluted by Congressional intervention, can be ignored during state and local implementation. Grodzins describes the situation:

[This dispersion of power and control] compels political activities on the part of the ad-

[74] Tyll van Geel, "Evaluation and Federalism," Special Qualifying Paper, Harvard Graduate School of Education, April, 1970, pp. 31, 34.

ministrator. Without this activity he will have no program to administer. And the political activity of the administrator, like the administrative activity of the legislator, is
often turned to representing in national programs the concern of state and local interests, as well as of other interest group constituencies ... always [the administrator] must
find support from legislators tied closely to state and local constituencies and state and
local governments. The administrator at the center cannot succeed in his fundamental
political role unless he shares power with these peripheral groups.[75]

What can be done?

Several steps can be taken to improve Title I. At a minimum, the program
needs better administration at the federal and state level. This will require more
people trained in management, evaluation, and program development. But
additional manpower may have only limited impact unless federal and state agencies gain greater leverage over local school districts. The problems of improving
Title I administration are complicated and cannot be totally resolved outside the
context of political change.

Creation of countervailing *local* forces to prod federal, state, and local officials
to act more forcefully may be the most important step. Efforts to establish strong
local parent advisory councils under the new federal guidelines could help produce more local responsiveness to the educational needs of the poor. Their demands for public accountability and a role in the development of programs could
increase the influence of the poor at the local level. But if strong local councils
are an important first step, greater organizing efforts aimed at the state and federal levels are also necessary. In Massachusetts, for example, the State Welfare
Rights Organization, community action agencies, the Harvard Center for Law and
Education, and other groups have recently banded together to encourage the
Department to issue strong guidelines governing local councils. On October 23,
1970, Massachusetts approved the most far-reaching guidelines of any in the
country.[76] They require each school district to set up election procedures immediately for as many parent councils as necessary to ensure representation from
every Title I school. Furthermore, the guidelines provide local advisory council
chairmen with the right of appeal to the State Commissioner of Education on
questions of Title I implementation. Such pressure may result not only in the
establishment of local councils, but also in the strengthening of the state's bar-

[75] Grodzins, *op. cit.*, p. 274.
[76] Memorandum from Neil V. Sullivan, Commissioner of Education, Massachusetts Department
of Education, to Superintendents of Schools and Title I, ESEA Directors, October 23, 1970.

gaining position with local school districts. No longer will the state be totally beholden to the wishes of local public schoolmen.

Similarly, community groups could band together on a nationwide basis, to bring pressure to bear on USOE and the Congress. Until recently, whenever USOE attempted to exert any influence, the only people they heard from were spokesmen for public educators trying to protect their own interests; typically USOE responded positively to this constituency. In the last few months, as we have seen, pressure has been coming from such groups as the Washington Research Project, the NAACP, the National Welfare Rights Organization, and they have had some success. But additional organization will probably be needed if such pressure is going to have a significant long term effect; many more poor will have to be organized for national pressure. In fact, chances of success may be greatest at the national level. Federal officials share with poor parents the distinction of being on the outside of our nation's school system. Assuming that some desire for reform remains in USOE, it is not inconceivable that it could work with the poor on some issues to force change on recalcitrant public school systems. For example, USOE and the poor probably have a mutual interest in increasing public school accountability for Title I. USOE has never used its broad authority to require good evaluation at the local level. Given a strong push by an effective lobby, USOE would be in a better bargaining position to impose this priority on public school educators.

This strategy of countervailing power, however, is not without its problems. For one thing, organizing effective parent lobbies around the fuzzy issue of "good education" is a formidable task. For another, there are many unresolved questions about the most productive relationship between professional educators and parents. How much parent control should there be? Who should make what decisions? What arrangements are in the best interests of school children? Finally, how would the Congress react if a lobby for the poor really threatened the established powers in education? Could the strategy backfire and result in the replacement of Title I with more general support for the schools? Merely raising these questions points out the risks and uncertainties involved in the development of countervailing local power. These uncertainties, however, must be contrasted with the near certainty of continued dilution of reform under the present balance of power. The expansion of local counter-pressures appears necessary and worth the risks if we are serious about translating the spirit of Title I reform into educational practice.

References

Allison, Graham T. *Bureaucracy and Policy: Conceptual Models and the Cuban Missile Crisis.* Boston: Little, Brown and Co., forthcoming 1971.

Bailey, Stephen K. and Mosher, Edith K. *ESEA: The Office of Education Administers a Law.* Syracuse: Syracuse University Press, 1968.

Beer, Samuel H. and Barringer, Richard E., editors. *The State and the Poor.* Cambridge: Winthrop Publishers, 1970.

Bendiner, Robert. *Obstacle Course on Capitol Hill.* New York: McGraw Hill Book Company, 1964.

Crozier, Michel. *The Bureaucratic Phenomenon.* Chicago: The University of Chicago Press, 1964.

Derthick, Martha. *The Influence of Federal Grants.* Cambridge: Harvard University Press, 1970.

Elazar, Daniel J. *American Federalism: A View from the States.* New York: Thomas Y. Crowell Company, 1966.

Grodzins, Morton. *The American System: A New View of Government in the United States.* Chicago: Rand McNally and Company, 1966.

Kaufman, Herbert. *Politics and Policies in State and Local Governments.* Englewood Cliffs, New Jersey: Prentice-Hall, Inc., 1963.

Meranto, Philip. *The Politics of Federal Aid to Education in 1965.* Syracuse: Syracuse University Press, 1967.

Moynihan, Daniel P. *Maximum Feasible Misunderstanding.* New York: The Free Press, 1969.

Munger, Frank J. and Fenno, Richard F., Jr. *National Politics and Federal Aid to Education.* Syracuse: Syracuse University Press, 1962.

Neustadt, Richard E. *Presidential Power.* New York: New American Library, 1960.

Sundquist, James L., editor. *On Fighting Poverty.* New York: Basic Books, Inc., 1969.

Educational Experimentation in National Social Policy*

P. MICHAEL TIMPANE

Washington, D. C.

The need for experimentation is clear. But in reviewing the history of educational experimentation—from Progressivism through the "Grey Areas" projects of the 1950's and the War on Poverty—the author suggests that fruitful experimentation demands a difficult balance of "real world" involvement and political insulation. The history is particularly relevant to an understanding of the origin, evolution, and prospects of the recent "Experimental Schools" Proposal.

On March 3, 1970, President Nixon sent to Congress the first formal message of his Presidency on the subject of education. Entitled, significantly, "Education Reform," this message emphasized the limited role of schools in solving social problems, the lack of order and demonstrated effectiveness in Federal education programs, and the absence of clear and widely understood techniques for improving the school learning process.[1] The most prominent of the President's proposed remedies for the shortcomings of America's schools was an expanded federal effort in research and experimentation in education problems. The nation's most needy students, the President argued, receive the least benefit from the public schools. Each year the gap between them and the well-to-do children

---

* The views expressed are the author's and do not represent those of the Department of Health, Education and Welfare.

[1] White House Press Release, "Message on Education Reform," March 3, 1970, p. 1.

Harvard Educational Review   Vol. 40   No. 4   November 1970, 547-566

widens. Until the nation knows what children learn and how specific educational practices make a difference in how much they learn, it would be unwise to pour new fedeal billions into the support of school operations. Instead, said Mr. Nixon, there should be established a National Institute of Education (NIE), to "begin the serious systematic search for new knowledge needed to make educational opportunity truly equal."[2] The NIE's priority tasks would be to determine if compensatory education of the poor can succeed; to find ways that all citizens can be taught to read; to explore the educational possibilities of television; and finally, to conduct a program of experimental schools.

This essay does not deal primarily with the President's assessment of American education (provocative though it be). Rather, it concentrates upon his acceptance of education as an appropriate arena for public experimentation at the federal level. The appearance of the "experimental schools" proposal in the President's program demonstrates, I believe, important themes in the recent development of American social policy:

1. A widening realization among federal social administrators, of both parties, that social action programs—or "laying on money in the name of doing good"[3]—do not always solve, or even always help solve, social problems.

2. The gradual realization among social scientists (and administrators) of the political dynamics of social research generally and social experimentation specifically.

3. A "return to basics" among would-be experimenters, in the sense of more careful attention to the requirements and limitations of experimental methodology.

This essay will review the antecedents of today's proposals for educational experimentation and, through an evaluation of their viability as social policy, will suggest the persistence of a fourth theme: namely, that social action programs and programs of social experimentation probably must, in the political nature of things, proceed side by side if either is to succeed fully.

Throughout, this essay refers repeatedly to experimentation, social experimentation, educational experimentation, and experimental schools. It will be useful to distinguish these terms at the outset. Briefly, "experimentation" here means a systematic effort to find the relationship between a treatment and a result: one defines the treatment and measures the result reasonably well, using

[2] *Ibid.*, p. 2-7.
[3] A phrase coined by Worth Bateman, (former Deputy Assistant Secretary of HEW for Income Maintenance and Social Service Planning) in "An Experimental Approach to Program Analysis: Stepchild in the Social Sciences." Paper delivered to the Operations Research Society of America, June 19, 1969.

a statistical design that allows one to control for other variables so that significant differences between treatments, or between a treatment and a non-treatment, can be identified. "Social experimentation" and "educational experimentation" are simply such experimentation conducted in the development or pursuit of social action programs and educational programs respectively. "Experimental schools" are a bit more difficult to define, since they have meant so many different things to so many people in this century. For the purposes of this paper they are defined quite arbitrarily as schools in which the "experimentation" referred to above was, is, or can be carried out and where the findings of that experimentation have or intend to have program policy implications. This definition includes what has been proposed by the President, but may exclude some other schools that have been called experimental.

The Estrangement of Experimentation and Education

To understand fully the development of federal experimental schools proposals, as well as the reaction to them among administrators and educators, it is necessary to trace two quite separate threads in American intellectual and social development. The first of these, namely the development during the past decade of a succession of related social experiments of national significance, may explain the development of the proposals; but it cannot adequately explain the reaction of many educators to them. For that understanding, one must delve into the peculiar history of American educational experimentation over the past century.

Early in this century, no word was more honored by American educators than "experimentation." The main current in the American philosophy of education was based squarely upon the pragmatism of William James and the experimentalism of John Dewey. These two had founded a uniquely American school of philosophy; and in so doing they, especially Dewey, drew from that philosophy many explicit applications to educational practice. All intellectual activity became, to them, a sort of experiment. In a continuous series of mental activities, each individual adapted to his changing environment, testing each attempted activity for its effect, accumulating an ever more well-informed consciousness. The questions of psychology became functional; how does the mind develop its values, its habits of operation, its "personality."

There flourished, under Dewey and the progressive educators who followed him, two widely different kinds of experimentation: the one rigorously scientif.c; the other often highly esthetic; the one centered in the laboratory; the other located in the field. Lawrence Cremin has termed these two developments in their extreme manifestations, "vigorous scientism," on the one hand, and "virulent sentimentalism," on the other.[4] Their common philosophical parentage was not, over the years, sufficient bond to hold these two streams of intellectual activity together; and in their drawing apart came, among other things, the drastic diminution of experimentation as a respected professional technique.

The scientists, typified by Edward L. Thorndike, sought a comprehensive science of pedagogy upon which all education could be based. As Thorndike said, "Everything that exists, exists in quantity and can be measured." Thus, through thousands of experiments and analyses conducted typically in a laboratory setting with a limited number of subjects performing highly defined activities, educational researchers set about "Wissenschaft with a vengeance."[5] By the 1930's, however, this movement was losing its vigor. For all the effort, results had been meager.[6] Edwin Boring concluded that experimentation had gained "a mass of knowledge about sensation . . . , a little else, and nothing of great moment about the rational mind, the personality, and human nature"[7]; and educational experimentation fell within his verdict. To make matters worse, the scientists of education had in their heyday floated grandiose claims of expected progress, and belittled nonexperimental wisdom. To them, educational progress was slow exactly because the scientific method had been too little applied. In the actual event, of course, most experiments were equivocal, or nonreplicable, or they simply confirmed prescientific wisdom. Over time, the experimenters lost not only their public, but their own morale.[8]

While the scientific experimenters were dwindling away, the field men were encountering their own set of difficulties. Their "experiments," too, were dying. At almost every large school of education—beginning with Dewey himself at Chicago in the 1890's—there had sprung up a laboratory school, where these imaginative educators could try out their theories, usually upon the children of the university faculty. Hundreds of private schools featuring similarly innovative methods were founded by the students of these men. But both these kinds of

[4] Lawrence Cremin, *The Transformation of the Schools* (New York: Vintage Books, 1964), p. 184.

[5] *Ibid.*, p. 200.

[6] Donald T. Campbell and Julian C. Stanley, *Experimental and Quasi-Experimental Design for Research* (Chicago: Rand, McNally and Company, 1963), p. 2.

[7] Edwin G. Boring, *History of Experimental Psychology* (New York: The Century Co., 1929), p. 659.

[8] Campbell and Stanley, *loc. cit.*

schools were characterized from the beginning by a lack of disciplined inquiry and a corresponding absence of well-substantiated results. The emphasis in most of these schools was promotional, to the neglect of hypothesis-testing. In the absence of any proofs of generalizable educational progress in them, the laboratory schools were written off by most educators as "too distinctive" to serve as models for the majority of the nation's schools. By the late thirties, the most prominent of the laboratory schools were closing their doors; and those that remained transformed slowly into conventional private schools for faculty children.[9] Many of the imitators among private schools folded or became, in time, those excesses of progressive education described by *New Yorker* cartoons and *Auntie Mame*.

Through both of these tales runs a theme of gradual estrangement of theorists from everyday practitioners and from other sources of public support. The theorists argued incessantly among themselves, whether education was a "science" or an "art." The original great men passed on one by one, and their less able successors retreated steadily behind the walls of university schools of education and private schools. The engagement of many of these men with popular front radicalism during the thirties further diminished lay support until, as something of a side effect of McCarthyism, the dynamic influence of progressive education, with its experimental bias, was ended. In 1959 when Merle Curti surveyed the intellectual scene in American education, he found no broadly based progressive force: only a lingering Marxism on the Left, a new emphasis on science and technology in the wake of Sputnik, and a widely popular fundamentalism promoting such axioms as "no fads and frills" and "back to the three R's."[10] Thus, entering the 1960's, the American educational establishment was in no mood to plunge into widespread school experimentation. Its heroes and mentors were dead, or tarnished, or both; its public support was fragile and conservative; as a maturing industry, its structure was increasingly bureaucratized and less susceptible to variation for the sake of research. By historical irony, when the time came for social experimentation in the 1960's, no major American social service was less ready to undertake the experimentation proposed and propagated by our great American philosophers than education, that service wherein they themselves had attempted it most extensively.

[9] Lee J. Cronbach and Patrick Suppes, eds., *Research for Tomorrow's Schools: Disciplined Inquiry for Education* (New York: The MacMillan Company, 1969), pp. 49-52.
[10] Merle Curti, *The Social Ideas of American Educators* (Patterson, New Jersey: Pageant Books, Inc., 1959), pp. xxv-xliv.

The "Grey Areas" Program: Linkage of Social Action and Research

Progressivism in American social thought had not, of course, been confined to educators. Since the nineteenth century, progressives interested primarily in social reform had been interested in education as a tool of reform. The focus of these men and women was much broader than the school, but the educational process in general and schools in particular were among the first and foremost instruments chosen to help achieve the social reform. Beginning in the 1950's, such reformers began to take up systematic experimentation as a means to solve the set of social problems afflicting the poor. During the 1950's, intellectual opinion in the social sciences began to coalesce around the persistent problems of poverty and increasing economic inequality amid affluence, and the persistent failure of urban renewal and other early nostrums to solve them[11] At the same time, there occurred what Moynihan has termed an "exponential growth of knowledge" in economics, statistics, and throughout the social sciences, accompanied by a greatly expanded number of social science and service professionals. Social problems became, to a degree never before approached, subject to expert judgment concerning their seriousness, likely persistence, and the level and kind of activity necessary to solve them. The first prominent convergence of these phenomena was promoted by the Ford Foundation in a series of projects preceding and comprising the "grey areas" program in the late 1950's and early 1960's. The Foundation's concern, and that of the many reformers that followed its efforts—in other foundations, in the President's Committee on Juvenile Delinquency, and in OEO and other federal agencies—was to promote substantial changes in the environment of the urban poor. To do this, the reformers relied upon improving the coordination of existing governmental and private services, and upon working directly with the disadvantaged and minority communities. Also, and most significantly for this paper, they proposed as an equally important aspect of their work, to "invent and evaluate new approaches in education, housing, employment, legal services, and welfare."[12]

Education was almost the first object of the new experimental attention. Even before the "grey areas" projects, the Ford Foundation had tried to attack city

[11] Daniel P. Moynihan, *Maximum Feasible Misunderstanding* (New York: The Free Press, 1969), pp. 1-36; Peter Marris and Martin Rein, *Dilemmas of Social Reform* (New York: Atherton Press, 1969), pp. 10-14.

[12] Paul Ylvisaker, Director of Public Affairs Program, Ford Foundation, quoted in Moynihan, *op. cit.*, p. 36.

social problems through large grants to several city school systems to help them respond to community conditions. But all soon realized that the schools were not able to change such conditions by themselves; and the Foundation itself had little clear idea of what it wanted done and no firm plan for testing the effectiveness of its efforts. These projects were termed "educational experiments," but they were really extemporized city-by-city. "Adopted sporadically, they lacked any logical coherence as a means of social betterment. Team teaching in one school, a pre-kindergarten in another, visits to parents' homes elsewhere amounted only to a rather capricious and inconsequential willingness to experiment. The value of the experiments was, besides, seldom thoroughly examined."[13] Little was expected, then, and little was gained. The Foundation moved on to its more ambitious "grey areas projects," where community action was to be born, without having yet learned the extent of the conflicts inherent in its developing concept of "action research."

In the grey areas projects, and in their companion projects funded by the President's Committee on Juvenile Delinquency, much more was expected. By now, the program managers had thought through their experimental strategy. Resources were to be concentrated upon a few large comprehensive projects which might claim wide relevance as demonstrations; and to prove this relevance, thorough objective evaluation would be an integral part of each project. As the projects were developed, educational innovations once again formed a significant part of each city's plans. In the attempt to implement these plans, though, much was to be learned about "dilemmas of social reform." For our purposes, two of these findings are most significant:

1. *The need for partnership with a public social institution to conduct experiments will skew experimental designs toward the more conventional, and will, during the experiment, raise up profound disagreements and misunderstandings as to what the experiment consists of and how it should be run.* The education components of the projects offer excellent examples of this problem. At the very heart of the "experiment" was the notion that things should somehow be done differently in the schools (specifically, by the teachers): thus, the project immediately threatened the key figures in its success. The professedly "experimental" character of the project could allay many of the initial fears of school superintendents, since results were, by prior definition, not assured and their prestige could thus hardly suffer; but no such alibi was afforded the teachers who

---

[13] Marris and Rein, *op. cit.*, p. 17.

were frequently already under attack by the community. The project managers' only recourse was to treat the teachers with kid gloves, and to install those innovations which offend teachers least. This amounted, in sum, to a "backing away from any radical change in the teachers' approach."[14] Even at that, there were continuing difficulties in the operation of the project, which often revealed that the superintendent's commitment and support was not so total as the project director had thought. What was the center of the project director's professional life turned out typically to be a rather marginal concern of the superintendent, a matter to which he was only nominally committed for the sake of the prestige it gave him and his system. In providing smooth administrative cooperation and timely support, the superintendent was frequently of little help.

2. *Within the responsibilities of the project director himself, the commitment to both demonstration and evaluation will create irreconcilable conflicts.* To demonstrate this conflict, one need only contrast the noble prospectus of Mobilization for Youth (MFY)—the most well-known "grey area" project—with Marris and Rein's description of how the experimental programs were actually run. MFY said in 1961 that it offered:

a broad program of action based on a coherent operating hypothesis and integrated with a carefully designed program of research and evaluation. Essentially, it is a project of social experimentation and investigation, using as its laboratory an urban residential area with a high delinquency rate, large and diverse enough in population to be representative of problem areas in many communities but small enough geographically to permit the operation of intensive programs of action and research.[15]

Looking back from the mid-60's upon MFY and its sister projects, Marris and Rein found a far different history:

The projects claimed to be experimenting, even when their actions were hardly consistent with the scientific method. Unproved ideas were borrowed and adapted from one project to the next, without controlling the variations in the interest of comparative analysis. Programs were introduced before the resources to evaluate them had been assured. The innovations to be tested were sometimes no more than the extension of well-tried practices. Eager to take advantage of new appropriations voted by Congress, the projects evolved their plans opportunistically, leaving research to hasten after money with as coherent an evaluative design as could be put together. Cities could not be treated as laboratories, ignoring their urgent need for all the resources they could attract. The

[14] *Ibid.*, pp. 58-67.
[15] MFY, Inc., "A Proposal . . . ," 1961, quoted in Moynihan, *op. cit.*, p. 52.

projects expanded according to the grants they could obtain, rather than the logic of an experimental progression.[16]

We should note two points from these contrasting passages. First, the need to act, to reform, conflicted seriously with the need to experiment and evaluate; and second, the need to reform won the battle if not the war.

The diminution of research by "action" demands in the grey areas projects is quite understandable. First, like John Dewey and his education colleagues a half century earlier, these reformers never really doubted the value of their "experimental" programs. The "experimental" design features were largely either rhetorical, to provide program flexibility, or instrumental, to provide a maximum proof of the program's effect. Their overriding concern was to bring social change, as rapidly as possible. Second, assuming (as was the fact) that the project administrator wanted to preserve as much experimental rigor as possible, he found at every decision-point that flexible action was typically much more rewarding than experimental purity. The staff, the cooperating institutions, the beneficiaries— whenever they had a preference, it was for progress or change, rather than enhanced experimental design. What is more, the experimental design was not a passive element in the administrator's calculations: it made incessant and substantial demands upon the resources available for other purposes and itself created conflict for him while promising him no political, and at best problematic intellectual, returns.

To decide that a project cannot have action and research goals at the same time, and to decide in favor of action is not, of course, to diminish the research need—the knowledge gap—that existed at the outset. The proper conclusion is to insulate research from action, and *vice versa*. Let the action portion of the programs be frankly "explorations of the possibilities of reform," freed from the demands of experimental design; and let the experimental research, where required, be what it must be—a scientific simplification of reality, detached, inflexible, hypothetical in the strict sense, and patient.[17]

The War on Poverty: Antecedents to the Experimental Schools Proposal

The conduct of the War on Poverty after 1965 reflected the lessons learned, unlearned, and forgotten from the grey areas experience. In the Office of Economic

---

[16] Marris & Rein, *op. cit.,* p. 192.
[17] *Ibid.,* p. 206.

Opportunity (OEO), research and demonstration were treated from the outset as separate interests, no longer integrated with every program. In the innovative action programs, much of the effort continued to be out-of-school education as in Head Start, Job Corps, and MDTA institutional training; but the research requirements associated with each program were considerably relaxed. The programs were evaluated *ex post,* selectively, and by contractors independent of the projects themselves. "Action managers" were not harnessed into experimental riggings. Nevertheless, between 1965 and 1968, in OEO and in the Department of Health, Education and Welfare, a succession of events (much too disparate to be called a series) combined—or conspired—to produce a new proposal for full-blown experimentation in the field of education—the "experimental schools" proposal. These events are so diverse and ill-related that they cannot be ranked by importance or from first cause to last effect. One can only list them in roughly chronological order.

1. *The spread of Planning-Programming-Budgeting (PPB).* From 1965 on, at the direction of the President, all federal agencies were engaged in implementing PPB; and none did so more vigorously than OEO and HEW. In addition to installing a more systematic planning and budgeting process, PPB had effects that enhanced the possibilities of experimentation. First it installed in the agency headquarters a sizeable staff of energetic academic social scientists (usually economists) who viewed decision-making with a critical and detached eye. What is more, they exalted the role of efficiency and effectiveness as proper criteria for decisions, and the contribution which systematic analysis could make to achieving these criteria.[18] Their primary impact on research and experimentation was to expand mightily the significance attached to program analysis and evaluation. From such emphasis there followed naturally an advocacy of experimentation, as a specie of *ex ante* evaluation.[19]

2. *The Head Start phenomenon.* Among the first programs proposed by OEO was Project Head Start, an effort to provide, to poor children, preschool assistance that might diminish their handicaps when they entered school. Project Head Start was originally conceived as an "experimental" program; but its history serves only to prove dramatically one of the basic shortcomings of experimental strategies—if a program is *too* attractive, political pressures will hustle it

[18] Charles L. Shultze, *The Politics and Economics of Public Spending* (Washington, D.C., The Brookings Institution, 1968), pp. 16-24.
[19] *Ibid.,* pp. 60, 125.

into operation whether or not the experimenters can provide theoretical justification.[20]

3. *The "planned variation" strategy of Project Follow Through.* Follow Through was intended to extend Project Head Start from preschool to the primary grades; but sufficient funds were not available at the outset to make it of comparable scope. Follow Through was converted forthwith into an effort to vary education strategies systematically. The Office of Education, which administers Follow Through, prepared a menu of project-types from which applicants would select the one most suitable to their circumstances, and an evaluation plan that would use common measures to assess all projects. Follow Through's impact on prospects for educational experimentation were several: it applied the notion of social experimentation to in-school education programs operationally for the first time.[21] But it demonstrated (and as an experiment, at least, foundered upon) the same old difficulties that we have seen before and will see again—the prodigious intellectual task of constructing theoretically sound experimental designs over a broad range of input, process, product, and environmental variables; and the political/administrative problem of enforcing controls sufficient to protect the integrity of the experimental design.[22] In this last respect, the Follow Through experience also pointed out that the line of control is greatly attenuated when a line agency of the federal government, dealing with a highly decentralized educational system, proposes to install such controls—rather than a private foundation, dealing directly with a community.

4. *The failure of education evaluation.* As we have seen, OEO program effectiveness was gauged not experimentally, but by independent *ex post* evaluations. Such was the case with Head Start; and such also the case with Title I of the Elementary and Secondary Education Act, an OE-administered billion-dollar social action program for the education of disadvantaged children. In 1968, program evaluations of these two programs brought in deeply disappointing findings—that neither was producing any remarkable enduring educational gains for the children. This disappointment was joined with the growing suspicion that Follow Through would not provide experimental results, and the conviction

[20] Walter Williams and John W. Evans, "The Politics of Evaluation: The Case of Head Start" (unpublished paper, CEPR Files, July 14, 1969), p. 7.

[21] Such an idea had been proposed by the President's Science Advisory Committee in the *Progress Report of the Panel on Educational Research and Development* (March, 1964), but it was not adopted until Follow Through.

[22] David K. Cohen, "Politics and Research: The Evaluation of Social Action Programs in Education," *Review of Educational Research*, April, 1970.

that even so excellent a survey as the Coleman Report could not supply definitive answers on how to improve the educational performance of poor children. Upon reflection, it seemed that some more rigorous investigation would be required to unravel such educational mysteries.

5. *The income maintenance experiments.* In 1968, OEO launched its most imaginative experimental project in the New Jersey negative income tax experiments. These experiments had two distinct effects on the course of educational experimentation. First, the notion that HEW should develop a program of experimental schools developed very much in conjunction with that department's involvement with the development of income maintenance strategies. By 1968, the PPB office in HEW was deeply involved in income maintenance planning, and in monitoring and expanding income maintenance experiments. Professional colleagues involved in both education and income maintenance planning pondered deeply the extent to which income maintenance experimentation had, even in advance of any experimental findings, clarified the issues and accelerated the development of viable proposals for welfare reform. Education evaluation having failed to produce such clarification, the conclusion that more controlled educational experimentation might was, in this bureaucratic environment, almost foreordained. And second, apart from its psychological impact upon education planners, income maintenance experimentation also produced the most careful analysis to date of the issues to be considered in the development of social experiments. Income maintenance planners took great care to confront the difficulties of public experimentation and to outline the strategy that a public experimental strategy must therefore pursue. As they saw it, the experimental method had major difficulties in public policy. Varying treatments for different people (i.e., the subjects and the control), raised questions of equity. Traditionally structured experiments were expensive, in time and money. And the methodology for social experimentation was little developed and largely untried. The tools of measurement were so crude that "Hawthorne effects" were often observed more easily than the effects of treatment variables. In view of such problems, they concluded that experimentation should be undertaken only in carefully prescribed circumstances:

"Experiments . . . are costly, technically demanding, politically sensitive, and difficult to administer. For these reasons it is essential that any such experiments supported by the government should provide information of high relevance to major policy questions, that such information be suitable for development through, and only through, the experimen-

FIRST CLASS
PERMIT No. 29764
BOSTON, MASS.

BUSINESS REPLY MAIL
NO POSTAGE STAMP NECESSARY IF MAILED IN THE UNITED STATES

Postage will be paid by

Harvard Educational Review

LONGFELLOW HALL, 13 APPIAN WAY

CAMBRIDGE, MASSACHUSETTS 02138

tal method, and that great care be taken that the experiments are rigorously designed, controlled and administered so that the results obtained are reliable.[23]

All in all, the theory and practice of the income maintenance experiments was, to a few key education policy-planners, an immanent demonstration of a newly sensible and promising approach to social experimentation.

6. *A New Administration.* When the Nixon Administration took office in January 1969, it brought a profound skepticism of the effectiveness of programs developed by its predecessor. It brought also a devotion to the virtues of efficient management, and an earnest desire to construct its own programs for social improvement. In education, these predelictions led it almost immediately to embrace experimental schools—conceptually developed but unbudgetted during the final months of the Johnson Administration.

One can, in fact, view the new Administration, and its initial attitude toward social programs, as personifying a skepticism and disillusion growing among social scientists and administrators during the later 1960's with the wisdom of swiftly expanding social service programs to overcome problems whose causes and cures were imperfectly understood. These themes have been presented recently by such critics as Lowi, Moynihan, and Banfield[24]: but it was sounded earlier *within* government, specifically by the men who had been most deeply involved in social experimentation. The Johnson Administration's evaluation chiefs in OEO wrote in mid-1969 that the 1965-vintage faith in action had led OEO to "push aside the fact that we had neither the benefit of experience nor much of a realization of the difficulties involved in developing effective techniques."[25] Similarly, the HEW planning deputies for education and income maintenance, both Democratic appointees, had concluded by about the same time, that "the flaw in the domestic policy of the Johnson Administration was that it depended on the assumption that spending money on education, job creation, training would lead to effective results. . . . The unfulfilled promise of ineffective programs has contributed to the awful malaise which this country suffers from now. People need

[23] President's Commission on Income Maintenance Programs, "Discussion Paper on Strategy for Income Maintenance Experimentation," July 6, 1969, pp. 1-8. These findings correspond closely to those drawn by the Institute for Research on Poverty, which studied these issues simultaneously, for HEW. See Larry L. Orr, "Strategy for a Broad Program of Experimentation in Income Maintenance," IRP *A Comprehensive Analysis of the Issues for Research, Demonstration and Experimentation in Income Maintenance* (Madison, Wisconsin, 1969).

[24] Theodore J. Lowi, *The End of Liberalism* (New York: W. W. Norton & Company, 1969).
Moynihan, *op. cit.*
Edward C. Banfield, *The Unheavenly City* (Boston: Little Brown & Company, 1970).
[25] Williams & Evans, *op. cit.*, p. 3.

to know that government can work and that implies . . . very careful structuring of governmental efforts, inaugurating large programs only after experiments have indicated success is likely. Otherwise, the cynicism, frustration and despair of the people in the country will grow."[26] The prominence of Moynihan and Banfield in Nixon Administration councils should be seen, then, as an intellectual as much as partisan turn-around in social policy perspectives.

The Experimental School Proposal

In the light, then, of seventy years of experimentalism in education and a decade of assorted impulses toward social experimentation, we can now turn to the experimental schools which President Nixon proposed this year.

In his first appearance before the House Committee on Education and Labor, HEW Secretary Robert H. Finch announced the Administration's plans. The experimental schools would, he said, identify and develop "successful approaches and promising new ideas in education." It would do this better than existing programs principally by designing experimental models encompassing whole schools, focusing the best ideas recently developed in education upon the most important social and educational issues, and by installing a system of thorough and rigorous documentation of the educational processes.[27] In terms of our experiment-or-exploration distinction, the Secretary's proposal was primarily "experiment." Already though, his statement reflected the political difficulties with such a proposal, for it will develop, he says, in partnership with State and local authorities.[28] This is just the first of the concessions to experience and reality which, in succeeding months modified and downgraded the program in Administration plans. The Secretary presented no further description of his proposed experimental schools to the Committee.

The first further explanation of what he had in mind came in July, 1969, with the circulation to the Congressional Committees of a lengthy descriptive memorandum.[29] In this memorandum, the experimental schools became two-stage op-

[26] John E. Brandl (formerly Deputy Assistant Secretary of HEW for Education Planning) memorandum to Assistant Secretary for Planning and Evaluation, Oct. 30, 1969, p. 4. Also see Bateman, *op. cit.*

[27] Secretary Robert H. Finch, *Statement before the Committee on Education and Labor,* March 10, 1969, p. 17.

[28] *Ibid.*

[29] (Office of the Assistant Secretary of HEW for Planning and Evaluation) "Experimental Schools," (July, 1969).

erations. They are still to be comprehensive and scrupulously documented; but realities have intruded a little more. In several months, the proposals had gathered little support. What support they had gained was based mostly on their innovative potential, not their experimental elegance. Accordingly, the innovative features have grown in prominence. The memorandum suggests that the experimental schools will first of all discover "whether it is possible to make dramatic improvements in educational achievement . . . —not in laboratories but in typical American neighborhoods and schools." This will be accomplished with innovative models of various already-promising developments, with rigorous but *ex post* evaluation. Later, planned variations will be introduced to "see if we can determine which particular factors do make a difference." The conditional tense of the second-stage experimental objectives reflects well the nature of the researcher's most effective objection to them. As the proposal now confesses, "we lack sufficient educational theory and sufficiently powerful statistical techniques to identify and determine the relative importance of the various factors influencing educational progress."[30] A problem lacking a theory for solution is not a good object for experimentation, so the income maintenance planners had said. Thus, the July proposal could claim that "the present state of the relevant social and statistical sciences is such that in the absence of large scale, scrupulously controlled education experiments we may not be able to identify productive approaches"[31]; but it could not make the necessary positive claim—that the presence of experimental schools *would* make that identification. What is more, faced with a response from the educational community ranging from apathy to hostility, the proposal added mechanisms to guard against the erosion of experimental control. Primarily, this took the form of seeking accountability through performance contracts with private firms. Such mechanisms were calculated not only to provide incentives to perform, but also to remove disincentives to evaluate and to offer insulation against the ever-present political pressures to water down the experimental design.

When Congress failed to appropriate funds for experimental schools for Fiscal Year 1970, another six months of planning became available to the new administration before the Legislature need be approached again. During this time, there was no backing away from the original analysis that the educational system needed to change and that more needed to be learned about how to change it. But there was further review of what needed to be done in research and innovation. By the

[30] *Ibid.*, p. 4.
[31] *Ibid.*, p. 5.

time of the President's Education Reform Message of March, 1970, the major research emphasis had shifted from experimental schools to devising new measures of achievement and to a National Institute of Education, which would coordinate "research and experimentation" (of an unspecified kind) generally. At the end of the message's research section lies one short paragraph on experimental schools; they are now one among several examples of research projects in the National Institute of Education. These schools are "highly important," the message says, "as a bridge between educational research and actual school practice."[32] Whether they are intended to be "exploratory" or "experimental" is wholly unclear. What is sure is that whatever their theoretical desirability, they had not gathered significant political and intellectual support and were less significant in administration plans than a year earlier.

The Prospects for Rigorous Experimentation

The viability of genuinely experimental schools as instruments of federal public policy remains to be demonstrated. Most of their predecessors in social experimentation have failed to produce experimental results, and the Administration proposals for experimental schools have themselves become successively less confident in their claims of how totally experimental these schools will be. It is clear that the experiments like those originally proposed in 1969—involving a whole school rather than some activity in it, as the object of the experiment—have never been attempted. *A priori* there are two obvious reasons for this: the methodological problems are very formidable, and the political realities of educational research have not encouraged such scope. Both reasons appear to be true.

Recent reviews of educational experimentation have portrayed a "state of the art" well below whole-school designs. One reviewer summed up the problem neatly in rudimentary cost-benefit terms:

There are expensive schools that are good schools; there are expensive schools that are poor schools. There are low-cost schools that are poor schools; there are low-cost schools that are extremely good schools. This highly confused situation is exactly what one would expect to find where there are a great many things that affect the quality of the schools. Many of these factors are independent of each other, and many others are tied together in extremely subtle ways.[33]

[32] White House Press Release, "Message on Educational Reforms," March 3, 1970, pp. 2-7.
[33] Harold F. Clark, *Cost and Quality in Public Education* (Syracuse: Syracuse University Press, 1963), p. 32.

Of the impact of experimentation upon this knowledge problem however, the same reviewer (and others) finds that most experiments have concerned a single aspect of education, usually one area of teaching method in a given subject, and that, cumulatively, such narrowly focused projects have "proven" a "wide variety of contradictory means" for improving learning.[34] Several inferences might be drawn from this result:

- educational progress is very difficult to measure.
- learning theory is presently too weak for the formulation of testable hypotheses and the construction of realistic parameters of variation—except in designs so limited that the results may not persist in non-laboratory environments.
- the experimental situation itself accounts for most of the measured variation (the Hawthorne effect).

It seems certain that educational research has not yet produced one of the important prerequisites of whole-school educational experimentation: a whole-school educational theory (or theories) of sufficient power and specificity to suggest the nature of the relationship one might hypothesize (and then test for) among the important educational variables. In this respect, educational experimentation seems to differ substantially from its income maintenance companion —where the economic theory of wages offers a quite solid basis for experimental design.

There are at least three ways to shape experiments that can occur in schools in ways that will make their success less problematic than the unqualified "whole-school" approach: 1) focus on a sub-group of the school population, 2) focus on areas of activity where previous research has offered the most promising leads, 3) simplify the experimental design to measure only a few key variables. This last step may corrupt experimental purity, but it will preserve the notion of systematic variation and could yield quasi-experimental results, superior to the information now available. This stance views each experiment, at any point in time as the first or n^{th} approximation of the optimal design of the experiment, subject to refinement at stated intervals in the life of the school. (Such a compromise might most appropriately be made for experiments which must, in their nature, be large scale, such as education vouchers or incentive payment schemes.) Not to be compromised, though, is the systematic application of the experimental

---

[34] *Ibid.*, p. 47. See also, J. R. Shannon, "Experiments in Education: A New Pattern and Frequency of Types," *Journal of Educational Research* XLVIII (Oct., 1954), pp. 81-93.

treatment. It must be conducted in many different environments which are representative of our nation's educational diversity.

Assuming that some such conceptual adaptations are made, any large-scale experimentation in schools will still encounter numerous administrative, political, and sometimes ethical problems (problems of non-manipulable variables and unforeseen effects) related to the establishment and control of the experiment.

Not least among these problems are the attitudes of administrators and bureaucrats. Most experiments (and for that matter, most comprehensive educational evaluations—the closest substitutes we have had for educational experimentation) have fallen into the "no significant difference" category. That is, the experimental group's results have differed little from the non-treated control. This is a respectable and even valuable scientific result, but it can be bureaucratic dynamite. Under the prevailing political ethic, a program or project is presumed to be doing well until proven otherwise. "No significant difference" can easily kill one program or project, to the advantage of others where there are no results at all—and this by virtue of measurements whose power and discrimination is little understood. In these circumstances the program operator's interests will be best served, in his view, by unproven but popular claims, not by carefully validated experimental data.

Before it is launched, experimentation must pass another difficult test. The administrator, be he President or Secretary or some more lowly functionary, must believe that the program decisions to be made require data of the quality offered up by experimentation. In education, this faith must encompass several arguable tenets. One must, for example, assume that there is a difference that education can make in children's achievement which it does not now make, if it is delivered in combinations which do not occur naturally. One must also assume that survey data on the present educational system, such as that collected by the Coleman Report, cannot, by any amount of statistical manipulation, provide good enough information—even though such surveys have rarely ever been done in this country, and though the Coleman Report alone has undoubtedly provided more policy-useful data than all educational experiments of this century put together. One would need to disagree with Moynihan's view that:

"Causal insights of the kind that can lead to the prediction of events are interesting, absorbing, but they are hardly necessary to the management of a large open political system. All that is needed is a rough, but hopefully constantly refined set of understandings as to what is associated with what."[35]

[35] Moynihan, *op. cit.*, p. 194.

Having surmounted all these hurdles, the would-be social experimenter in education would still not be home free. He would still have to face what the history of the past ten years suggests is the most basic dilemma of social experimentation: *If a problem area proposed for experimentation is unpopular and/or unimportant, experimentation should not and/or will not be done; but if it is popular and important, action will not wait for experimentation.*

What, then, may we conclude about the viability of educational experimentation generally and the experimental schools proposals specifically, as instruments of social policy? It is clear that experimentation in schools could contribute badly-needed knowledge about the processes by which many of our people succeed or fail as students and as citizens. It is equally clear, though, that such experimentation must be carefully shaped, to fit the state-of-the-art in educational research, and to "fit" with the political rewards systems of educators, bureaucrats, and elected political officials—which systems are, in general, inhospitable to experimentation. To be realistic, the experiments must occur in real schools, but to be manageable they must, at least to start with, be of modest scope; they must be systematic in applying the same treatment in several different environments. The experiments should deal with important policy issues affecting acknowledged problems in our society (the financing and delivery of education to poor children fits this prescription beautifully.) But they must be separated from and supportive of, but not unnecessarily competitive with, other programs of action and exploration in education.

It is this last point which suggests our escape from the persistent dilemma. The early history of social action and experimentation argues that insofar as experimentation is separated from social action, it may, for its narrowness, suffer from lack of relevance and lack of support. The more recent history—the grey areas projects and the early Head Start experience—argue that we must insure some separation or the action interests will diminish experimentation and its desired products drastically. Too much insulation and too little insulation both reduce the likelihood of fruitful experimentation.

The proposed National Institute of Education—removed from the Office of Education—may, by its position in the national government, be able to satisfy the difficult requirements for separation and linkage. But history hardly offers ground for boundless optimism! Nor does the scarcity of resources improve the promise. In the competition for funds, short-term attention to action demands is likely to offer greater promise of political reward than research.

In the present setting, then, a rationalizing process such as experimentation is desperately needed, and just as desperately doomed (with all its built-in handicaps) itself to gain influence by the same slow process as its more saleable companions—be the process called log-rolling or "muddling through." Political wisdom seems, then, to dictate quite limited reliance on experimentation, or any other single tool, to the exclusion of other techniques the decision-maker must use to scratch around the educational barnyard. While we act and explore, we must also experiment; while we experiment, we must also act and explore.

On Tuition Vouchers:
An Essay Review

MARY JO BANE
Harvard University

EDUCATION VOUCHERS by the Center for the Study of Public Policy. *Cambridge, Massachusetts. Final Report, December 1970. 348 pp.*

PRIVATE WEALTH AND PUBLIC EDUCATION by John E. Coons, William H. Clune III, and Stephen D. Sugarman. *Cambridge, Mass.: Harvard University Press, 1970. 520 pp. $12.50.*

AN ESSAY ON ALTERNATIVES IN EDUCATION by Everett Reimer. *Cuernavaca, Mexico: Centro Intercultural der Documentacion, 1970. 89 pp.*

Reforming the financing and administration of public education may be an important step in reforming education itself. But no administrative schemes—community control, state-wide financing, revenue sharing, performance contracting, or vouchers—are panaceas. Voucher plans, which would give parents chits or scrip worth a certain amount of money to "spend" for their children's education at any public or private school, have received a good deal of attention recently, as a result of the release of the CSPP report and the possibility that a field test in one community will soon be funded by the Office of Economic Opportunity. The strange collections of people who have lined up on both sides of the voucher debate illustrate an important fact: inherently, vouchers are neither radical nor conservative. They can be espoused, for different purposes, by such different people as Milton Friedman, white southerners, and Ivan Illich.

Reading *Education Vouchers* in conjunction with *Private Wealth and Public Education* and *An Essay on Alternatives*[1] raises broad questions about the use of administrative and

[1] This essay is the first draft of a book on Alternatives in Education which will be published commercially in 1971. It is to be the subject of a seminar at Cuernavaca during the spring of 1971, during which the ideas in the essay will be further developed. In this review, the essay is discussed primarily as its ideas relate to voucher proposals. It is inappropriate to review a first draft, and I do not attempt to do so. (Reimer's book is paginated by chapters. The citation, "p. 1/2," refers to page two of chapter one. All references are given in this form.)

Harvard Educational Review Vol. 41 No. 1 February 1971, 79-87

financial mechanisms to work toward a more equitable distribution of educational resources and a more diverse and flexible set of educational offerings.[2] *Education Vouchers* is basically a practical document, which suggests policies and procedures for establishing a voucher system which would accomplish some redistribution of resources and would provide some choice among schools for parents. The proposed system would allow vouchers to be "spent" at any school meeting minimum state requirements. Schools would be forbidden to charge tuition in addition to the value of the voucher. The vouchers of the poor would be worth more to a school than the vouchers of the rich, thus encouraging schools both to enroll more poor children and perhaps even to spend more on their education.

Vouchers and Equality

Equality of Educational Opportunity is an overworked and probably meaningless term. Coleman showed to most people's satisfaction that the amount of resources devoted to a child's schooling has little effect on his performance. But equality of opportunity apart from concrete resources cannot be defined, much less provided; and equality of performance is a goal few would consider practical or even desirable. Educational resources are at present distributed inequitably. Reallocation from the rich to the poor is certainly a necessary, though few would argue a sufficient, step in efforts to reduce social class biases in education.

Private Wealth provides an impressive analysis of the present inequities in educational spending, before going on to outline an "apparatus for justice." Education is now financed primarily by local property taxes, supplemented by state and federal funds. Because some local school districts are more wealthy than others, equal efforts by the residents—as manifested in equal tax rates—may result in extremely unequal funds available per pupil. Inequalities in wealth are compounded by the fact that certain districts, notably

---

[2] The issues of redistribution of resources and provision of diversity and choice are not, of course, the only aspects of the voucher debate. The most public discussion has been generated by the questions of segregation and of aid to religious schools. The voucher plan proposed by *Education Vouchers* includes procedures for preventing discrimination and a lottery admissions system to insure equal access to desirable schools. The authors of the report expect that these procedures will not produce any more racial and social class segregation than the present system, and may well produce considerably less. The religious issue depends primarily on the courts' interpretation of the first amendment and various state statutes, which are now being reviewed in the context of certain states' purchase of services legislation. Presumably these two issues can be settled by regulation or ruling by the courts. Another source of opposition to vouchers, and the largest stumbling block to a field study, is the organized education lobby—NEA and AFT. Their opposition is partly self-interested, in that it may be harder to bargain with individual voucher schools than with a centralized district. However, their main objections seem to be ideological—that a voucher system would "destroy the public schools." They do not seem to have carefully considered the possibility that this might be a good thing.

cities, may need to spend a larger proportion of their tax income on other services than schools, for example higher costing police and fire services.[3]

State aid plans, which return some portion of state revenues to local districts, have not significantly reduced inequalities among districts. Some state aid plans use flat grants, which provide equal per pupil subsidies to all districts. Although these plans may raise the absolute level of per pupil spending in poor districts, they do almost nothing about the relative levels of spending in rich and poor districts. Other state aid plans, called "foundation plans," establish a basic level of per pupil expenditures for the state, and then supplement local revenues in order to bring district expenditures up to that level. Such plans are more equalizing than flat grant plans, but there is one major limitation, their tendency to be set at approximately the average per pupil expenditure for the state. This means that perhaps half the districts in the state are still able to spend more than the others, since no foundation plan in any state involves taking money away from rich districts. Setting the foundation high enough so that no district will want to exceed it is possible (it has been done in Utah) but is probably politically impossible in states which have a greater range in the wealth of districts and a greater desire for diversity in educational offerings.

Deciding what to do about inequities is not so easy as documenting their existence, and neither *Private Wealth* nor *Education Vouchers* offers completely satisfactory answers. *Private Wealth* proposes that the state take over the financing of education and distribute its revenues to districts or to families on the basis of the effort they are willing to expend in support of education, as evidenced by the rate of tax they are willing to pay. *Education Vouchers* assumes that much of the financing of education will remain at the local district level, supplemented by state and federal funds. Its system would distribute the revenues to schools, on the basis of their pupils' family income, with schools getting more money for poor pupils than for rich. In considering these plans, three questions must be examined: 1) at what level should revenues be collected and aggregated for equitable distribution? 2) to what units should the revenues be distributed? 3) according to what criteria should distribution occur?

If economic equalization is the criterion, it is clear revenues should be collected and aggregated for equitable distribution to the highest level at which it is administratively and politically possible. *Private Wealth* assumes that for the present this is the state level, although mention is made of the desirability of federal equalizing of state wealth. *Education Vouchers* does not consider the question in any detail. Its reliance on district financing, supplemented by state and federal funds, takes inadequate account of Coons'

[3] This is an extremely important cause of unequal spending on schools. Inequalities in the wealth of districts are, as a matter of fact, almost uncorrelated with inequalities in the income of residents due to odd distributions of commercial and industrial property. This fact makes the calculation of equitable formulas for distributing funds somewhat more complicated than Coons allows. Effort would have to be calculated in terms of taxation rates for schools, not general taxation rates, to be fair.

analysis of the limitations of existing state "foundation plans" and the failures of Title I.

Private Wealth, Education Vouchers, and *An Essay on Alternatives* agree that revenue should be distributed to the smallest unit which is administratively and politically possible. *Private Wealth* first discusses equalizing by districts, allowing each district to determine the level of taxation it is willing to impose upon itself and the type of educational offerings it desires. In a later section of the book, and in an article proposing equalizing legislation,[4] however, Coons suggests that the family is the more appropriate unit for making such choices. *Education Vouchers* concurs; *An Essay on Alternatives* suggests that the individual, especially as he grows older, should have the power to choose his own education. Advocates of community control (and NEA/AFT) argue with this "answer" and raise the important issue of where the locus of educational decision-making should be. Whether the family or the individual knows what is "best" is unclear, although the present state of education indicates that their judgments can hardly be worse than those now made by the professionals and the state.

The question of criteria for distributing resources is more adequately analyzed in *Education Vouchers* than in *Private Wealth.* Coons *et al.* assume that effort, i.e., what percentage of its income a family is willing to sacrifice for education, ought to determine resource allocation. *Education Vouchers* examines this and other criteria before arriving at its own suggestion: need defined as family income. The first criterion considered in the analysis is wealth: this is the basis for the present distribution of resources. Rich districts spend more; rich parents can, if they wish, send their children to expensive private schools. A voucher system which could be supplemented by private funds would have the same effect. The model is rejected by both Coons and CSPP. A second possibility is equality; each child would receive a voucher worth the same amount. However, this criterion does not take into account the special needs of students whom the public schools find more difficult or more unpleasant to educate. This model is rejected by *Education Vouchers* because it does not take these needs into account. It is rejected by *Private Wealth* because it limits the choice of schools offered to parents—they cannot choose schools which spend more or less than the established level. The effort criterion is examined and rejected by *Education Vouchers* because it would discriminate against those children whose parents were uninterested in education. The fourth criterion, and that adopted by *Education Vouchers,* is "need." Its proposals would make the vouchers of the poor worth more than those of the rich. Although income does not define *educational* need, the more relevant measures (e.g., IQ and behavior characteristics) are almost impossible to apply and tend to correlate with income for those groups of children for whom it is important. (See analysis in Chapter 7 of the Final Report.)

Any voucher proposal ought to be examined carefully in the light of all three of these

[4] John E. Coons, "Recreating the Family's Role in Education" in *Inequality in Education,* Harvard Center for Law and Education, March 16, 1970.

questions, since choice of the wrong levels or the wrong criteria for distribution could exacerbate rather than alleviate present inequities in resource allocation. "An unregulated voucher system could be the most serious setback for the education of disadvantaged children in the history of the United States" (*Education Vouchers*, p. 17).

Vouchers and Alternatives to Schools

Thus far we have considered the question of allocation of "educational resources" without defining the term or asking which individuals and groups ought to be considered legitimate providers of resources. The commonly accepted assumption is that educational resources are those things provided by and located in schools. Although a moment's thought leads to the conclusion that books, television, and big brother taking the kid for a walk are also educational, funds for education continue to be allotted solely to schools.

It is now familiar practice for schools to try to make their curricula more "relevant" and more "meaningful" by utilizing a diversity of materials and experiences to supplement the teacher and the text. More and more schools incorporate audio-visual materials, programmed instruction, games, and field trips into the child's learning experience.

Reimer's book, *An Essay on Alternatives in Education,* extends this principle by examining the concept of educational resources apart from the institution of the school. He argues, based on experience in underdeveloped countries, that the only way to provide *education* for all is to provide it outside of *schools*. He says, "No country in the world can afford the education its people demand in the form of schools" (p. 1/2). The cost of building high-quality schools for all in under-developed countries is a prohibitive diversion of resources from other services. The problem exists even in the United States, in a somewhat different form: "Continued attempts to supply the demand for college study in the United States will condemn the black and rural minorities to an indefinite wait for an adequate education" (p. 1/2).

The historical response to the problem has been to school the elite, excluding others by more or less subtle mechanisms. Tracking, evaluation procedures, testing, and differential curricula exist along with differential drop-out rates and high correlation of academic achievement and social class. But the problem of the schools is not only that they do not provide for all: they do not provide a proper education for anyone. "We need alternatives to schools not only so that all men can share in education, but even more so that men can learn freely what they need to know for their secular salvation" (p. 1/6).

Schools now perform, according to Reimer, four social functions: custodial care, social-role selection, indoctrination, and "education"—development of skills and knowledge. The first three functions conflict with the fourth, and result in the school's being a truly inefficient institution for education. The custodial care provided by the schools is extraordinarily expensive and diverts resources from education. Ironically, the supply of custodial care creates its own demand: "Schools provide child-care for younger children which they prevent older children from supplying" (p. 2/1). The school's function of carrying out social-role selection conflicts directly with its educative function. Continual evaluation and sorting, while useful for stratification, is detrimental to motivation. Training is carried on inefficiently, in school vocational programs rather than on the job; education becomes elitist. Indoctrination is harmful in that the school teaches that the teacher is the source of knowledge and must be pleased; that "learning" is carried on in an uninteresting and orderly way, according to a fixed schedule; and that docility and conformity lead to success.

The schools' monopoly of what we define as educational resources results in inefficient use, because they are diverted to other functions which conflict in many ways with that of education. Separating the concept of educational resources from that of schools leads us to consider new ways of performing the functions now performed by schools, and to consider whether the functions now performed by schools ought to be performed at all. Reimer proposes that we search for alternative institutions for performing the function of education: "Alternatives must be more economical than schools, cheap enough so that everyone can share in them. They must also, however, be more effective so that lower costs do not imply less education . . . The schools system must not be replaced by another dominant system; alternatives must be plural . . . Education should not be separated from work and the rest of life, but integrated with them. Educational environments should be protective only to an unavoidable degree. Education should not, primarily, prepare for something else nor be a by-product of something else. It should be a self-justified activity designed to help man gain and maintain control of himself, his society and his environment" (p. 6/1).

Let us imagine vouchers which were not just for school, but for education. We might envision a lifetime account for each individual equal to the average amount now spent on schools. The vouchers could be spent at any time during a person's life for the use of a wide variety of educational resources organized in diverse ways. The account might be used for renting instructional materials for use in the home, or for paying the teacher of a neighborhood-organized mini-school. A group of families might get together and buy math materials or simulation games. A young adolescent might use part of his account to buy a place as a research assistant and trainee in a scientific laboratory. He might himself be paid for accompanying younger children on exploratory nature walks.

The job of a "board of education" under such a system would be to organize resources. This could not be left to chance, because sophisticated instructional technology should not be abandoned in favor of "learning at mother's knee." The board would operate a library of books, films, records, programmed materials, games, etc., for use in homes and neighborhood centers. It could recruit adults to teach reading, to utilize young assistants in an office or lab, to conduct seminars on music appreciation, or simply to walk and talk with children. It could match available adults with children who desired a particular kind of education, and could provide space and materials for their use.

The voucher plans discussed above tackle one problem in the allocation of educational resources—to provide reasonably equal access for all. Following the proposals of Reimer, they might be broadened to tackle another problem—to provide resources for efficient education, both within and outside of school:

> Thus, even the first step in equalizing educational opportunity among social classes requires an allocation of educational resources outside the school system. The only ways of making sure that poor children get even their fair share of public funds for education are either to segregate them completely in schools of their own or to give the money directly to them. The first of these alternatives has been tried and failed. The second provides a key to the allocation of all educational resources (p. 9/7).

> Concrete alternatives to schools neither can nor should be specified. To do so would violate the most important principle stated above, namely that control of educational resources should be in the hands of the persons seeking to learn. Only a few general principles should modify this control, and these to insure that educational resources are as plentiful and as well distributed as possible. These principles are easily summarized. Educational time and space and the objects and human resources required for education should be as broadly defined as possible, as nearly identical with all human time and space, all objects and all people. Public resources for education should be equally shared by and under the control of individual learners (p. 9/9).

Neither the Coons nor the CSPP plan envisions "education vouchers" in Reimer's sense. It is possible, of course, that "schools" will be defined very loosely by whatever agency has the responsibility for determining who is eligible to cash vouchers. In this situation, vouchers might be a first step in education's moving out of the schools and into more diverse settings.

Vouchers have the potential for working a radical change on the educational system by challenging its procedures for defining and allocating the resources people can use to learn. But they will certainly not fulfill this potential without a corresponding change in society's attitudes toward education and toward the economic and social institutions which utilize the stratification system of the schools. Thus, the important question for those interested in substantial change is a tactical one: are vouchers likely to help or hinder necessary changes in attitudes?

Several questions must be considered. The first is how a voucher system is likely to work, once put into operation. Will procedures be incorporated into the system and enforced which improve the present distribution of resources and insure more equal access to "desirable" schools? Will "schools" be defined broadly by those determining eligibility, or will even more restrictions than now exist be imposed? What will the tendency of the voucher administration be over the long run—will it become more regulatory and more centralized than when it started, or more free? Will the politics involved in passing enabling legislation for a voucher system mitigate all its good features?[5]

---

[5] It is impossible to say much about these questions although California's experience with a voucher bill, The Elementary Demonstration Scholarship Act of 1970 (Assembly Bill #2471),

A second question is whether the free enterprise model is an appropriate one for public services. Vouchers are being considered for financing not only education but also such diverse services as day care, housing, medical care, and transportation. Questions can be raised in each area about the efficiency of competition, the dangers of inappropriate advertising, and the tendency for private enterprise to concentrate on profits rather than quality services. It is certainly possible that many of the dangers can be avoided by intelligent regulation. It is also possible that there are subtle dangers which have not yet been considered, for example, a tendency to reinforce certain general attitudes toward public services. Vouchers imply that all services should be paid for by individuals; free provision of services implies that some things belong to the community and are free for use by all. Deciding which attitude set might be more healthy for our future well-being is extremely difficult.

A more specific question is whether a voucher system would be abused by profit-makers. The experiences of colleges and private schools suggests that the control of education by big business equipped with advertising and manipulation of public opinion in search of profits may not be a danger, although the issue demands careful consideration before a scheme is enacted. It is possible (although perhaps unnecessary, as the profit margins of colleges show us) to confine voucher cashing privileges to non-profit institutions. It is equally possible, however, that blurring the distinction between private enterprise and public service may be useful. Education and housing, in our tradition, are both public and private. They are public in that the community feels a responsibility to provide them for its members; they are private in that they affect the well-being of the individual and ought, in some way, to be under the control of the individual. Vouchers may provide a way for the federal government, which has the best apparatus for collecting revenues on a progressive scale, to put these revenues in the hands of those who need them. The federal government itself seems to be notoriously inefficient at administering social services; revenue sharing with lower levels of government has not solved the problem. Putting the money for services in the hands of the people, with power to choose among various providers of services might, with proper regulation, be a flexible and powerful mechanism for income redistribution and for imaginative approaches to public service.

The third question is whether supporting a voucher plan is a good tactic for bringing about change in education. Many would argue, along the lines outlined above, that vouch-

---

provides some clues. The draft legislation waived state requirements on class size, curriculum, minimum schoolday, and certification requirements for voucher schools. It excluded profit-making schools, but allowed religious ones. It required public access to financial and administrative records, and periodic reports on the progress of pupils as determined by standardized tests. It also required that schools "offer a comprehensive course of study in the basic skill areas of reading; mathematics; and the English language, whether as a second language or the language of instruction; "and that they prohibit instruction in unconstitutional areas, such as the violent overthrow of the United States or California." The bill was supported by Ronald Reagan. It was killed in committee by the Masons.

ers are a positive step in the direction of reforming the educational system. There are also those who argue that voucher financing is merely a way of shoring up a failing school system, which needs to be abolished in toto and replaced with a flexible system of educational alternatives. Others oppose vouchers because they do not do the whole job of redefining and reallocating educational resources. Such positions are not merely the manifestation of a "revolutionary" as opposed to an "evolutionary" approach to social change. Individual analysis of the empirical issues in the context of a theory of social change may lead to different positions by thoughtful men as well as by self-interested groups. Deciding "whose side are you on" is not so easy as it looks.

An Interview with James Allen *

JAMES E. ALLEN, JR.

Washington, D. C.

In this frank interview, the former Assistant Secretary and Commissioner of Education discusses his tenure in Washington. He points to several promising initiatives. But with regard to the poor and the blacks, he identifies the Nixon administration strategy as one of minimal accommodation, not leadership or advocacy; and regrets the inadequate financing of education by the federal government and a "continuing and serious under-estimation of the degree of alienation and disaffection of the young." As matters of structural improvement, he recommends the National Institute of Education and the elevation of Education to Departmental status.

As the Assistant Secretary for Education and the United States Commissioner of Education, what role did you seek to play?

Between the date that the President appointed me and the date I took office, I gave a great deal of thought to the mission of the Office of Education and to what the priorities should be. I felt that one of the things that was needed was stronger leadership by the Office of Education in the development of policy within the government; that is, the office should become a more vigorous and influential advocate for change and relevance in American education. My observation had been that the Office of Education was becoming more and more an agency composed of disparate units too heavily preoccupied with the administration and distribution of federal funds. In recent years the office had grown

* Interviewers were Richard Darman and Gregory Thomson of the HER Editorial Board.

Harvard Educational Review   Vol. 40   No. 4   November 1970, 533-546

rapidly, primarily in response to Congressional action, with the specific responsibility of its various units closely related to a particular piece of legislation.
There was a lack of cohesiveness and of clarity as to goals and priorities. I
was not interested in joining the office merely to serve as the chief administrator
of a collection of check-writing units. I sought a more direct impact on the development of American education and hoped to achieve this by getting the Office of Education to begin to think and act as an *advocate* for change and improvement.

What goals did you set in attempting to carry out this role?

It seemed to me that there were three things that the Office of Education ought
to be concerned with as general goals. One was to take the lead in developing
a nation-wide strategy for maintaining a continuing process of improvement
and relevance in American education. A second goal was to accelerate the process
of eliminating failures in the educational system, particularly with respect to
the disadvantaged and all those who suffer a lack of motivation, physical and
mental handicaps, and discrimination. While the government had already started
on this process, it seemed to me that the Office of Education ought to be more
actively concerned with seeing that programs work more effectively, advocating
their expansion where necessary and promoting the use of federal resources to
the fullest extent in eliminating failures. The third broad goal was to ensure a
more effective distribution of governmental resources in relation to educational
need. Only the federal government can provide for the equalization of resources
among the states, and it has a direct responsibility for doing so.

The nature and dimension of this responsibility are well demonstrated by the
current need to bring both the provision and the distribution of federal resources into line with the drive for social justice. For example, the whole question of eliminating segregation in education is one in which the federal government should serve not only as an advocate, but also as a facilitator by seeing to it
that the necessary resources are made available in the right places and at the
right times.

*The second goal that you mentioned was to be an advocate of change by elimi-
nating failure. How did you attempt to fulfill this?*

It was in conjunction with this goal that I proposed the nation-wide Right to
Read effort. It seemed to me unthinkable that at this stage in our history we
should allow any boy or girl to leave school without having acquired the skills

to read; and yet one out of four was leaving school without these skills. Here was an area of advocacy where the Commissioner of Education and the Office of Education could say to the country and to the educational forces: "Look, here is something that we can no longer tolerate. Let's get at it! Let's eliminate this deficiency." This doesn't mean that the federal government and the Office of Education either can or should take total responsibility, but certainly there can be leadership at the federal level to marshal the resources of the entire country to help the states and localities with the elimination of reading deficiencies. I was told after I made the speech calling upon the country to eliminate deficiencies in this field that this was the first time a Commissioner of Education had advocated such action. Other commissioners had advocated legislation and money to deal with specific problems, but none had ever taken a particular curriculum area and, setting both the target and the timetable, challenged the country and the educational system to do something about it. This is what I mean by the Office of Education's being more of an advocate, initiating action rather than merely somewhat passively carrying out legislative mandates.

What progress do you feel you made in regard to your main goals?

Progress was slow because it's very difficult to move the Office in this direction in view of all the forces—of size, complexity, established practice—that work against change.

With respect to the Right to Read program, the staff of the Office of Education was enthusiastic and there was an enormous amount of favorable response throughout the country, particularly from the private sector. There seemed to be a readiness to accept guidance and leadership in this area, indicating to me that, if the Commissioner of Education spoke out, he could have an influence far beyond the dollars that might be involved.

The first goal, linking the processes of change—research, development, evaluation, dissemination, etc.—to achieve a continuous improvement and relevance, stimulated the proposal for a National Institute of Education. The President has adopted this proposal and it is now in the form of legislation which will, I hope, be approved by the Congress.

The interest of the Administration in channeling available funds more in the direction of the disadvantaged was in part, I think, a response to our efforts to be an advocate for change.

Finally, the appointment by the President of a National Commission on School Finance, headed by Mr. Neil McElroy, was in direct response to my recommendation that we attempt to put the system of financing public education in order. The federal government's responsibility in the financing of education includes not only the provision of its rightful share in the support of education, but also encouragement for the states to put their own schoolhouses in financial order. Such an updating of state school finance plans is essential for achieving an effective and equitable distribution and use of our total resources for the support of education.

It sounds as if you may have been less frustrated as Commissioner of Education than some have suggested.

These were important steps but there was frustration, for in terms of the realities of the times and the enormity of the educational task, they were relatively small steps. For example, I came hoping I could initiate a vigorous program in urban education and I hoped to see large sums allocated for a more concerted and systematic attack on the problems of the inner-city schools. The task force on urban education appointed by Secretary Finch came up with a report advocating substantial monies—something like fourteen billion dollars over five years—for urban schools. This report was obviously coolly received by an Administration concerned primarily with inflation and keeping the budget balanced.

It soon became apparent that there would be no large-scale immediate action in this area and that hopes for a major attack on urban education and for substantial increases in funds for other purposes would have to be brought into accommodation with both the need and the Administration's emphasis on building into the educational system better capacity for reform and renewal.

The Nixon administration was very much interested in reform. For one thing, it did not require, at least immediately, large sums of money. There was also a genuine feeling, which I shared, that we were at a point in history that called for some reappraisal. Through the fifties, education was primarily concerned with the provision of the teachers, the buildings, and the general growth necessary to meet expanding enrollments. Through the sixties, the emphasis shifted to a concern for the disadvantaged, the blacks, the poor, with the creation of all sorts of new programs to deal with their special needs. At the end of the sixties starts had been made in many directions, but there was a growing recognition of the need for evidence of their effectiveness. For example, despite many encouraging signs of success, the available information about the effects of Title I and certain other parts of the Elementary and Secondary Education

Act was insufficient to provide the hard evidence required for justification of large additional funds.

Hence, there was a widespread feeling within the Administration that the time had come to pause, examine, and evaluate before proposing large new investments.

How did you react to this philosophy?

I was sympathetic with the basic premises of this position. For years I have been calling for educational reform, recognizing that such reform could be sound only if based upon better knowledge of what works and doesn't work. Consequently, during my tenure as Commissioner, I was active in supporting increased funding for educational research and development and such projects as the proposed National Institute of Education. But I could not agree that increased support for education could await the realization of reform. There are many good things going on in the educational system and these deserve adequate financing which can be achieved only with the help of the federal government. Hence, on May 5 of this year, I wrote the President urgently requesting a higher priority for education in planning the budget for the fiscal year 1972 and recommending a public commitment to an allocation of one billion dollars over and above the present ceiling for HEW, to be used in several critical areas: early childhood education, the Right to Read, education for the handicapped, vocational education, institutional aid for higher education, and environmental-ecological education. In justifying this request, I made the point that children cannot be put in "deep freeze" to await the development of a better way to educate them. I indicated also that I could not, in faithfulness to my concern for education, continue for a third fiscal year to defend budget proposals which I considered to be insufficient federal support for education in these critical times.

What response did you get from the President?

I never received a response to this letter. I had some general comments from the staff in the White House, some saying it was a good letter, others saying it was impossible to respond to it at this point. I had tried to make it known in the letter that I felt that there was a good deal of disenchantment in the country, particularly among educators, with respect to the commitment of this Administration to education. No matter how much I tried to sell the National Institute of Education, the Commission on School Finance, and other Administration initiatives, I couldn't generate much enthusiasm from an educational community feeling that it was drowning in a rising tide of financial problems. In this situation educators were interested not so much in discussions on how to swim but rather in being rescued and turning the tide.

Are you suggesting that you would have traded additional inflation for more funding of education, or would you have preferred taking the increase of one billion dollars from some other ongoing programs.

I recognized that curbing the trend of inflation was in the best interest of the country at this point, and also in the best interest of education. After all, if additional money is going to be consumed merely in keeping up with rising costs, it doesn't do much to improve education. So I was in favor of trying to curb inflation. But it seemed to me that in a two hundred billion dollar federal budget, education simply ought to be granted the higher priority that would bring it a larger proportion of these funds.

To what do you attribute the lack of responsiveness on the part of the Administration to your proposals?

I felt that what was lacking was a sense of urgency with respect to education, and that in the absence of this sense of urgency educational decisions and policies were shaped more in terms of the fiscal constraints than in terms of the nation's educational needs. The vast influence of those persons in the White House and in the Bureau of the Budget who were dealing with education was exerted primarily in terms of economic goals.

What does it take short of resignations and the closing of four hundred college campuses to get a message of urgency from the educational community through to the President?

I wish I knew the answer to that question. Basic, of course, is the degree of receptiveness to the concerns of education on the part of the President and his Administration. While an interest in education had been expressed, I never felt that this interest went so far as to constitute a commitment either sufficiently deep or perceptive to be translated into the scope and kind of action that seemed to me to be necessary. It was unfortunate that the concerns of the college campuses did not really receive serious consideration in the White House until after Kent State and Jackson State and the march on Washington of May ninth. Had there been earlier a more serious effort to understand the young people and their concerns, I think the Administration would have been less surprised by the reaction to the Cambodian decision and more sympathetic to the college presidents who were being charged by some with being too soft on students and unable to cope with difficulties on their campuses.

It would seem that the events of these recent years both on and off college campuses would have revealed the fundamental nature and the strength of the social movements of our times, particularly with respect to students and blacks and that the message of urgency would have been self-evident. But despite signs of a growing receptiveness, there are indications of a continuing and serious under-estimation of the degree of alienation and disaffection of the young toward their government and society. The education community continues to face the dual task of trying to guide protests into peaceful expressions and of pressing for action by the Administration that will begin to correct the conditions which are at the root of the unrest.

Is it possible to be both sympathetic to the interests of the young and the blacks and to wage war in Vietnam?

In practical terms, the answer is probably yes, but in terms of the viewpoints of many of the young and the blacks to whom this question relates, the two issues are mutually contradictory.

Aside from the difficulties presented by the war, do you discern a Nixon administration strategy for dealing with problems of the poor, the blacks, the disenchanted?

In my opinion, the principal strategy of this Administration is one of accommodation, that is, of going only so far as is necessary to keep as many different people as possible placated. In and of themselves, many of the proposals and many actions of the Administration such as the Family Assistance Program, the desegregation efforts, and the program of aid to economically disadvantaged college students are good, but they are not good enough as solutions for problems which threaten the existence of our country and test our commitment to democratic principles. It seems to me that what we need from the Administration in power at this critical period in our history is not mere accommodation but leadership that captures the imagination of the people, appeals to their best instincts, and generates a widespread conviction of the necessity of eliminating the longstanding prejudices, discriminatory practices, and injustices suffered by the poor, the black, and the other neglected groups in our society.

I am writing you directly to express my very deep concern over the critical needs of education in our country and our Administration's current posture towards them, and to urge the immediate adoption of a more aggressive program of action in the 1972 budget planning cycle.

*   *   *

Reform cannot be achieved in a vacuum. The system of education must be sustained and nourished at the same time change and innovation are sought. The children and youth in school today, or those about to enter, cannot be placed in "deep freeze" while desired change is awaited; the on-going operations of the institutions which provide for the education of these children and youth cannot be allowed to stagnate or deteriorate while the institutions are being expected to undergo fundamental reform.

*   *   *

I respectfully request, therefore, that you approve now—and publicly announce—an allocation to HEW for education in Fiscal Year 1972 of $1 billion over and above the total dollar ceiling presently allocated to HEW programs for that year to be used for new initiatives in the following areas. . . .

May 5, 1970 (from a letter to President Nixon)

Obviously, my professional competence cannot include questions of this sort. Thus any opinion that I have is only a personal one, like that of most other citizens. I find it difficult to understand the rationale for the necessity of the move into Cambodia as a means of supporting and hastening the withdrawal from Viet Nam—a withdrawal that I feel must be accomplished as quickly as possible.

What concerns me most now is what our responsibility is in dealing with the disastrous effects that this action has had on education throughout the country and on the confidence of millions of concerned citizens in their Government.

May 21, 1970 (reply to a staff member's question)

At five o'clock yesterday afternoon at a meeting in his office, Secretary Finch informed me that he had been directed to request my resignation as Assistant Secretary for Education in HEW and United States Commissioner of Education. I have this morning submitted my letter of resignation to the President.

Much of my experience as Commissioner of Education has been rewarding and satisfying, but difficulties and conflicts have been apparent from the beginning of my tenure. Foremost among these have been the serious frustrations and discouragements in trying to carry forward the drive to eliminate racial segregation in the schools and to obtain a priority for education at the federal level commensurate with its importance and its urgent needs. Of special concern also has been the inordinate influence of partisan political considerations in the matter of appointments to positions in the Office of Education. . . .

June 11, 1970 (statement in connection with dismissal)

. . . Let us then dedicate ourselves anew to supplying the missing ingredient—a sense of urgency. Let us be possessed by it, and let us make ourselves heard. . . .

July 8, 1970 (conclusion of a speech to the Annual Meeting, Education Commission of the States)

But how about such "New Federalist" policies as revenue sharing, voucher payments, and block grants?

These methods of funding can be important parts of the total effort to provide adequate financing for American education. I favor some form of revenue sharing, especially if earmarked in whole or part for education. I also support the concept of block grants.

In general, I see the federal government as having three roles to play with respect to educational finance:

1) *general support*—either through revenue sharing or block grants;
2) *categorical aids*—to pinpoint attacks on special areas of need (e.g., handicapped children, economically disadvantaged groups, vocational education, etc.); and
3) *funds for educational research and development*—to seek out, evaluate, and disseminate programs and techniques for improving educational practice.

With respect to the "voucher system," I have encouraged and supported the use of federal funds to explore its potential as a way of seeking new approaches to education. While I am not prepared to endorse the voucher plan at this time, I think it is an idea that needs to be tried out.

What response would you make to those who claim that, regardless of the general factors working against blacks, American education is racist?

Generally speaking, I think the *intent* of American education is not racist but in *operation* it often is, because it provides blacks, by and large, with inferior education. It has been generally structured and developed to serve the middle and upper-middle classes so that, in practice, our system of education is unresponsive to the needs of the blacks and tends to foster prejudice and discrimination, and is thus, in that sense, racist.

What hope is there for changing this kind of system?

Certainly there is more hope now than ever before because we are at last acknowledging the racist-producing features of our system and are seeking to eliminate them. We are also recognizing that these features exist because of neglect of the fundamental obligation and task of education, which is to provide equality of educational opportunity for all, and that the change required is the action necessary to achieve this goal.

Is part of the difficulty in promoting change the fact that the White House has taken policy-making initiative away from the Office of Education?

The White House has not *taken away* policy-making initiative from the Office of Education. The opportunity for initiative is still very much present, but in question is the influence of the Office on final policy decisions. The Office can and does make proposals, submit plans, and develop budget requests. But the way things operate, there are many inputs that affect policy other than those from the Office of Education. The Bureau of the Budget, the Secretary of HEW, the various units in the Secretary's office, the President's Science Advisory Council, the Council of Economic Advisors, staff assistants in the White House, and many others get into the act, so that any Office of Education proposal may be just one of many. This multi-mind approach also operates in the process of the evaluation of proposals. In the final analysis, of course, the decisions are made by the President or by those in the White House who speak directly for him. The result may not always be best for education because the ultimate decision may be highly affected by political considerations.

There was a suggestion that your dismissal stemmed from your inability to manage the Office of Education. Is the Office manageable?

Of course the Office of Education is manageable. It is a smaller agency in number of people, in breadth of responsibility, and in budget than the New York State Department of Education over which I presided for fourteen years. The real difficulty of managing the Office of Education stems from its position among the centers and forces within the federal government. The Office is just one among many agencies that deal with education, and many forces play upon it—from the Secretary's Office, the White House, the Bureau of the Budget, and elsewhere—and these complicate its management. Operating in such an entanglement of intra- and inter-agency relationships and pressures hinders the attainment of the three basics of efficient management—competent people, a clear sense of mission, and involvement in key decisions.

Why was it difficult to recruit personnel for the Office of Education?

Recruitment of personnel for the non-civil service positions in the federal government is of course always affected by the reluctance of some to go into what would in all probability be a short-term situation and by the misgivings about the stultifying effects of bureaucracy. But despite these negative attitudes there are many good people willing to serve in the Office of Education. My experience in Washington reaffirmed an earlier conviction that the stereotype of a "bureaucrat" is seldom a reality. I was tremendously impressed with the dedication and ability of USOE employees. They worked hard, often without recognition and frequently under totally unrealistic timetables, to serve the government and the nation. I was especially impressed with the loyalty given to me and the willingness and desire of many young employees to work within the system to achieve a better society.

Immediately after my appointment by the President, I set up a committee of distinguished individuals to recommend people for the vacancies in top-level positions in the Office. Although the number of "Schedule C" positions I could fill was far fewer in proportion to the total size of the Office than was the case in New York State, I had more such positions available to me than did my predecessors because I was serving as Assistant Secretary for Education in HEW as well as U.S. Commissioner of Education. This committee gave me a very fine panel of candidates who were enthusiastic about coming to the Office. When I began to recommend people from this panel for appointment, however, I promptly met with what was to be one of my most serious frustrations in operating as Commissioner—the necessity for political clearance. This requirement was foreign to my fourteen years experience in New York State where I was able to fill all top-level positions without interference in regard to political considerations. While I realized of course that the Washington scene would be more political, I was unprepared and dismayed to find that political considerations weighed so heavily. Equally frustrating was the inordinate delay in the clearance process which would sometimes stretch into months. Such partisan political influence is accepted as a condition of employment, a fact of life in the federal government, but for it to be of such paramount concern is, I believe, unfortunate in the field of education. It should be possible to select people for the Office of Education solely on the basis of competence without regard to political affiliations. Educational policy and operations at any level of government should not be subject to the unsettling and possibly regressive effects of swings of the political pendulum.

Did political considerations apply to research people as well?

Yes, but research also presents other special problems. When I looked for people to head the Bureau of Research, the unit for Planning and Evaluation, and the like, it was very difficult to attract first-rate people. Those who were in research or had research experience were most often in universities where they had more freedom than would be possible in the Office of Education with its Civil Service requirements and all the other bureaucratic trappings that go with a government agency. Some who were approached told me that they held research contracts with the Office of Education which offered both more money and more opportunity than would a position in the Office.

Is there no way to attract these people?

It seemed to a number of us who were considering this problem—and who were eager to strengthen and expand educational research at the national level—that the creation of the National Institute of Education would be a good approach. Placed outside the Office of Education, yet within HEW under the Assistant Secretary for Education, given freedom from the limitations of Civil Service requirements and other bureaucratic restrictions, such an Institute could attract top-level research talent for short periods of time or on a permanent basis. It is conceivable that the National Institute might develop some programs of personnel exchange with the Office of Education for the benefit of both. As envisioned, the Institute would be guided by distinguished representatives of various parts of the educational community—predominantly people from research—through a board of directors or other policy body.

You prescribe an organizational restructuring for research. Is a reorganization appropriate for other policy-making problems to which you've alluded—particularly those involving "political considerations"?

When I say political considerations, I am, of course, talking about partisan political considerations. Obviously education and politics have to be working together. The question is how education can be set up at the federal level, how its policy-making machinery can be structured to minimize the effects of partisan politics and special interest groups. This is a serious problem now and a big challenge for the future.

You've suggested that New York's climate, in this regard, was more favorable. Why?

In New York State, the Education Department is a separate Constitutional agency under the Regents of the University of the State of New York. The Regents are elected by the Legislature, one each year for a fifteen-year term. The Governor has no direct say in their selection or in their policy-making functions. The State Education Commissioner is appointed by the Regents without regard to politics and serves at their pleasure. He must, of course, work with the Governor and the Legislature but his administrative actions are not subject to their direction. He is insulated against partisan political pressures in a way not possible in the Washington structure.

In Albany, I was not a part of the political administration; I had much more freedom to speak in terms of what I believed was best for education. In the federal government, there is no individual, there is no agency which can speak for education without regard to political or special interest considerations. While the Legislature and the Governor in Albany may have made their final decisions by balancing what was best for education and what was politically desirable, at least there was an agency that could speak out publicly at all times on all issues solely in terms of education's welfare. In Washington, it is expected that regardless of circumstances the Commissioner's public statements will support the policies of the Administration in power.

Would you extend the New York model to the federal government?

In principle, yes. I would like to see eventually a major change in the structure for education at the federal level. I favor a Department of Education. Elevation of the Office to this status would certainly provide a sharper focus for the development of national educational plans and policies, but such a move of itself would not suffice. Department status would still leave education subject to the uncertainties of political currents. It would be well to consider also, therefore, some type of national board. Its structure would, of course, have to be carefully devised but it should encompass such features as lay membership, presidential appointment, overlapping terms to guard against undue influence of any one Administration. The power of such a board would not of course be the same as those of a state board, but they should be of the character and the degree necessary to provide stability and insulation for education policy making—insulation, on the one hand, from partisan political interference, and, on the other, from special interest groups.

You say "eventually" . . . ?

There is growing sentiment throughout the country for some kind of change in the legal structure for education at the federal level. I intend to develop further my thoughts on this subject in the months ahead.

As the country becomes more concerned about education, as the sense of urgency increases, and as federal participation in education continues to grow, the need for a sharper definition of the federal role will be emphasized. This clearer understanding of the federal role in education will, I believe, provide an impetus for beginning action on securing this long considered change. Presidential commitment to this goal would of course be essential.

Notes on Contributors

James E. Allen, Jr. is currently Lecturer on Education and Public Affairs at Princeton University. Dr. Allen is the former U. S. Commissioner of Education and Assistant Secretary for Education in the Department of Health, Education, and Welfare. Prior to that he served as Commissioner of Education and President of the University of the State of New York.

Mary Jo Bane is a doctoral candidate at the Harvard Graduate School of Education, a consultant to the Center for the Study of Public Policy, and a teacher in the Brookline Public Schools.

Richard L. Berkman practices law in Boston.

David L. Kirp is Assistant Professor at the Harvard Graduate School of Education and Director of the Center for Law and Education. His published articles include "Community Control, Public Policy, and the Limits of Law," which appeared in the *Michigan Law Review* in June, 1970.

Jerome T. Murphy is a doctoral student at the Harvard Graduate School of Education, concentrating on organizational theory and the politics of education. Previously he served as Associate Staff Director of the National Advisory Council on the Education of Disadvantaged Children and as Associate Director of the White House Fellows Program.

P. Michael Timpane is Executive Assistant to the Assistant Secretary for Planning and Evaluation, Department of Health, Education, and Welfare. During 1968-69 he participated in the staff development of the experimental schools proposal. He prepared the article appearing in this reprint while he was attending the Kennedy School of Government, Harvard University.